50 Spiritually Powerful Meditations

50 Spiritually Powerful Meditations

Dr. Margaret Rogers Van Coops
Ph.D., DCH (IM)

JAICO PUBLISHING HOUSE
Ahmedabad Bangalore Bhopal Chennai
Delhi Hyderabad Kolkata Mumbai

Published by Jaico Publishing House
A-2, Jash Chambers, Sir Phirozshah Mehta Road
Fort, Mumbai - 400 001
jaicopub@vsnl.com
www.jaicobooks.com

Published in arrangement with
Sumaris Center
321 Farallon Drive, Lake Havasu City, AZ 86403, U.S.A.
sumaris@sumariscenter.com

50 SPIRITUALLY POWERFUL MEDITATIONS
ISBN 81-7224-624-2

First Jaico Impression: 1997
Ninth Jaico Impression: 2008

Printed by
Snehesh Printers
320-A, Shah & Nahar Ind. Est. A-1
Lower Parel, Mumbai - 400 013.

Dedication

This book is dedicated to my parents,
Aubrey and Pat Pogson,
without whose love and support
I would not have lived this life to its fullest.

TABLE OF CONTENTS

How To Use This Book

Your spirit is the dimension where self touches God. Contained in that dimension is a sense of your true destiny, your true nature and purpose. The **50 Spiritually Powerful Meditations** in this book will assist you in gaining awareness of your true nature. This awareness will attune, unify and focus all your powers and energies. When you are attuned to your true nature, your life in all its details flows more spontaneously, more freely, and more successfully. When you are so attuned, your spirit attracts and harmonizes the energies of your conscious and subconscious minds with the deep subconscious that is your spirit mind. Your deep subconscious self knows all truth about everything you have experienced no matter what form you have previously taken.

Self-knowledge is the first step in the process of transformation. It is the goal of each individual to move beyond the egotistical self and its illusory appearance and unveil a true identity that is spiritual. Every time a false identity is surrendered, the vacuum it leaves is filled with spiritual insight that reveals wisdom. When we consciously align ourselves with the Universal Wisdom of the Creator, we become self-realized, enlightened, and harmoniously balanced. We begin to live unconditional love. No matter what happens in the outer world from this point on, the inner self is undisturbed.

Meditation is a tool you can use to actualize more of your potential, achieve greater personal harmony, solve daily problems and encounter new experiences in consciousness.

It is also an exercise in attaining a higher level of wisdom and awareness. This awareness brought forward from your deep subconscious (spirit mind) will unify and focus the power and energies of your conscious and subconscious minds. When this occurs, you will be able to manifest aspects of the Universal Consciousness. Energy absorbed from the Universal Consciousness (superconsciousness) will manifest itself in your daily life. Meditation can be practiced with many goals in mind. The meditations in this book cover self-improvement, therapy, healing and pain control, as well as esoteric, metaphysical practices, such as channeling, chakra clearing, astral traveling, cutting etheric ribbons, and much more, for there are no limits to the development of the mind.

The first stage of meditation concerns only the physical body and its normal functions. Here you must learn to know every inch of yourself and value your body as a sacred temple, for it is the house in which your spirit lives, and your spirit is an important part of God deserving love and respect.

The second stage deals with the understanding of your conscious mind, which often rationalizes against the true self that is your spirit. You will learn to control argumentative thoughts that arise from the conscious mind until that part of you becomes silent. Once silence is attained, the next level can evolve.

The third stage is that of attuning to your subconscious where all memory of your emotional and mental experiences in this life have been stored for examination. Careful study will reveal positive and negative mindsets that have created joy or sadness. By allowing an assimilation of these experiences to flow into the deep subconscious, the fourth stage can evolve.

The fourth stage involves attuning to your deep subconscious, or spirit mind, where your true self can be revealed.

Once you have reached the fourth stage and attained balance through the acceptance of your body, mind, emotions, and spirit, your psyche will fall into place naturally. It is at this stage that you can choose a personal direction to follow that will bring fulfillment into your life.

I was fortunate to be born with a well-developed psychic ability that naturally opened communication with my spirit guides and master teachers. They lovingly supported me in my quest to know about them and the world of spirit. As my enthusiasm grew, they advised me to follow their instructions step by step. They gently showed me how steeped in fear I was—from previous lives as well as this life and the worlds between. Through meditation, with their help, I faced my fears and finally found acceptance of myself and my life.

Though there have been literally hundreds of meditations given to me by my spirit guides, I have carefully selected these 50 meditations for their powerful effectiveness. Your own spirit guides will be there to help you, too.

Read the instructions in this chapter before using any of the meditations. Practice the basic meditation technique in this chapter until it becomes second nature. This will guarantee successful results with the other meditations. I will also give you some tips on recording the meditations on tape so you may use them over and over.

BASIC RELAXATION MEDITATION

This technique will be the first step in any meditation you will use. Once you have become thoroughly familiar with this technique, you'll be able to achieve a state of relaxation within seconds.

It is essential to work in a quiet room, free from interruptions. Choose a time and place where you can be comfortable, quiet and undisturbed. You may play soothing meditation music, if you desire. Remove any restrictive clothing, such as belts or ties.

Sit upright, with your back well supported, legs stretched comfortably before you, and hands resting gently on your lap or beside you. Or you may lie on your back, aligning your body in a north/south direction, head north, hands resting beside you.

With your eyes closed, sense your body's weight. It should be evenly distributed. If not, move until the weight feels equal all over. Once you are comfortably settled, tell yourself you will not move, no matter what physical senses occur. These physical manifestations are disruptive thoughts from the conscious mind to prevent you from proceeding. They are caused by the conscious mind's fear of the unknown.

Begin breathing slowly, easily, deeply. Inhale, hold your breath for a moment or two, then exhale with a sigh. Repeat this breathing pattern again, using a slow, even rhythm.

Ask the Higher Power for spiritual protection, using a prayer of your own choosing. I have included the one I use at the end of this meditation.

Envision a bright, white light above your head. This is the Universal Light of Life Energy, the God Light, which then pours over your head and runs through your entire body. Know that this white light is removing all stress and tension. Watch it move slowly through you. Constantly see the light and tell yourself that the tension is leaving you through the soles of your feet, and is moving away from you into the ground where Mother Nature uses it to rejuvenate the earth itself.

When your body feels light, stay in this state until you sense it is time to return. When you are ready, open your eyes. Sit up slowly with knees bent or, if already sitting, move your body slowly.

Say a prayer of your own choosing, thanking the Creator. Then, congratulate yourself on a meditation well done.

The following are some of the things you may feel and experience which are normal while doing this meditation. Remember, you need have no fear and should accept these things as normal.

- When you first relax into the meditation, you may experience a compulsion to fidget with hands and body.
- Your mind may chatter constantly.
- Itching, sneezing, pain, difficulty in breathing, swallowing, panic, tingling, prickles, heaviness, feeling light-headed or dizzy, are likely to occur at one time or another. Tell yourself these are distractions. Give in to them only if too compelling. This means ending the meditation immediately. You are not ready to proceed. Remember, practice makes perfect. Be patient and loving with yourself.
- Contradictory feelings—big and small, light and heavy, narrow and wide, light and dark, hot and cold—may occur, along with good and bad thoughts. Accept them and observe them. If you feel compelled to stop, do so.
- Fear arising from the unknown may produce swells of energy from the stomach and heart areas. If you can observe them, the feelings will dissipate and you can continue, but if you feel compelled to stop, do so. To proceed would achieve nothing.
- You may hear yourself breathing. It may sound as though someone is breathing in your ear. This is normal. It is the sound of your breath heard from within your head. If you find yourself running short of breath and being afraid, cease the meditation at once, for you are facing fear. If you can be objective and move through fear, then continue to face the fear until it subsides.
- Body sounds, such as stomach growling, are normal. These sounds will increase as your meditation skills

grow. Your heartbeat should become slower. If it becomes faster, you must decide whether to face whatever fear is surfacing or cease the meditation.

- You may experience sensations of intense cold or heat. This is normal. You may either move into this space and stay with it or move through it.
- Tingling sensations in the hands and feet are indicative of stress energy leaving your body, as are any skin sensations, such as tightness, numbness, and chills.
- Feelings of uneasiness, as though being observed, suggest unfriendly forces. Slowly end the meditation.
- Swirling sensations are an indication of out-of-alignment energy moving in the five bodies—physical, etheric, spirit, mental and soul. Think of these five bodies as one and the spinning should cease. If the spinning continues, causing you to feel sickly or nauseated, cease the meditation.

Note: The purpose of this meditation is to return to normal consciousness with a true sense of well-being. It takes time to learn to relax, so take the time.

SPIRITUAL PROTECTION PRAYER

"Oh God, Creator of all things, I ask that I be embraced and encompassed by your love; that I reside in the comfort of your protection from all things seen and unseen, all negative forces and elements that may threaten me. I surrender myself to your will and willingly receive your light that will uplift my soul and enable my will to become one with yours. In love, I reach out to receive your messages of truth through my spirit guides and I thank you now for the healing that will be given to me. Also, I ask for your healing light to flow through those people who are in my life. Help them to know you in me as I aspire to be your emissary. So be it."

As I say this prayer of protection, I visualize a white beam of light flowing over me. I allow myself to sense its presence as it flows into my body. I then visualize a second beam of light, golden in color, flowing over me. This second beam is then absorbed into my body.

I affirm that I am filled with the power of Spirit and the divine essence of unconditional love. I then visualize these two beams of light blending within me and watch them flowing out from my body, creating an auric field in the shape of an egg, which extends some three feet from my body in all directions.

MAKING YOUR OWN MEDITATION TAPE

If your mind tends to wander, it may help to make your own, personalized tape. Keep in mind that you don't want to have to turn your machine on and off during meditation, so include all the steps: lying down, closing eyes, breathing, progressive relaxation, and so on.

Practice the meditation before recording it so you will know how long to make the pauses between steps. Allow enough time to complete each step before moving on to the next. You may include the Basic Relaxation Meditation at the beginning of each meditation, if you wish.

You may choose to read the meditation as it is written or you may add your own embellishments, such as affirmations or mantras. Address yourself as "you" on the tape, as if you were hypnotizing yourself. When recording, stand or sit up straight, make yourself comfortable, and speak slowly and evenly in a clear, normal tone. You may include soft, soothing meditation music in the background, although this may cause problems if you need to edit or rerecord portions of the tape. If you want to add music to your meditations, I recommend playing the music softly in the background while you listen to the tape.

Meditation To Control The Conscious Mind

1

Your conscious mind is quite frequently a liar and cheat. It has no conscience and will do anything to maintain its power over you and keep the old mindsets running. Over time, you will re-educate this part of yourself, teaching it to listen to and learn from your Higher Self, and eventually to understand the true meaning of wisdom. When practicing this meditation, always be patient with yourself.

- Once you are relaxed, begin to observe how often your thoughts drift into daily worries and other distractions, day-dreaming, or falling asleep. (If you fall asleep, you will end the meditation. This is not unusual in the beginning.)
- If your mind flows into worries and fears, do not contemplate them—merely observe them as interesting and note your body's reactions, such as muscle tension.
- Acknowledge the stress you have created within your body. Mentally visualize this stress as thick black oil.
- Visualize the white light above your head. Watch it pour over you, pushing this oil down your body and out through your feet into the earth. Continue in this manner to observe your worrisome thoughts and the corresponding bodily reactions until you feel you have had enough. (Your body will tense and relax many times during this stage of the meditation.)
- Consciously relax again and allow yourself to recognize how your conscious mind prevents you from true relaxation. Take several deep breaths, and with each breath, allow yourself to relax more and more deeply.

- Allow yourself to contemplate any new realizations that you may have discovered about yourself. Affirm to yourself that you will work with them for the betterment of self. Breathe deeply three or four times.
- Return your mind to the bright white light above your head and allow yourself to visualize a safe haven where you can go to begin work on your new discoveries. Know that this place is special for you and that your Higher Self will always help you when you journey there.
- If you find yourself drifting into aimless daydreams or sleep, bring your mind back to the body and notice the tension you have created within the body as you have drifted. Recognize that your conscious mind has taken control. Do not be angry with yourself. Breathe deeply and pay attention to any tense areas that have manifested and ask yourself why. Wait and observe the answer that arises. Allow your Higher Self to release this tension by attuning once more to the white light. Watch the tension leave through the soles of your feet.
- Visualize your safe haven as you continue the meditation.
- Allow your Lower Self to absorb the healing energy that this place gives you. Give your conscious mind permission to daydream as a reward for facing truth. (You will drift into meaningful dreams where your conscious mind will make the necessary adaptations. Later, with regular practice, you will find yourself able to stay in a concentrated state where you can explore yourself more fully.)
- If you do not fall into a deep sleep, gently return to full waking consciousness and write your findings down. If you do fall asleep, write your dreams down for future reference and interpretation.

Note: With practice you will be able to eliminate a great deal of the unnecessary tension and stress your body has carried from old, undesirable mind sets.

Meditation To Close The Chakras

2

In our normal everyday life, the lower chakras help us feel our way through life. If our chakras are wide open, others can drain our energy. It is important to know how to close your chakras and protect yourself from others. Practice this meditation as often as you can.

- Sit or stand comfortably. Take several deep breaths and relax.
- Become aware of your genital area, which is the location of the Root Chakra, and gently contract the muscles. As you do this, visualize a large ring reducing in size until it becomes a small dot. Relax the muscles.
- Attune to your Solar Plexus Chakra. Pull your abdominal muscles inward slowly, visualizing the same ring growing smaller until it has become a small dot. Feel the tension you have created there, and recognize this tension as your form of protection. Relax the muscles and breathe deeply.
- Now become aware of your Heart Chakra. Breathe deeply. Pull your chest in as you breathe out, at the same time visualizing the ring becoming a small dot. Take several breaths and relax your body.
- If your throat aches, you will need to close your Throat Chakra. Swallow many times, allowing yourself to visualize the ring reducing to a small dot. Breathe deeply and relax the muscles around your neck and jaw.
- If your third eye is open and you are not using it properly, you will have a headache. Breathe deeply and allow yourself to

frown profusely as you visualize an eyelid closing down over an iris. Breathe deeply and allow the tension to leave your head.

- Your Crown Chakra should always be slightly open, so that you can be in contact with God and your Spiritual Teachers. Allow yourself to visualize the ring and ask yourself if it is closed or open enough. Your initial feeling is the right one. Gently rub the top of your head as you visualize yourself correcting it.
- Your Spleen Chakra should always be balanced. To correct any fault, allow yourself to visualize some small scales. If the pans are not hanging level, adjust them by placing something into one of the pans. As you visualize the pans becoming level, pull your left side muscles in and sense this chakra closing.
- Now become aware of your Crown Chakra once more. Let yourself attune to God and receive his love as the white light flowing throughout your body. When this is done, attune to your hand and foot chakras and visualize four small rings, all reducing to spots. Clench your hands and feet as you do this. Relax and breathe deeply. You are ready to face the world.

Note: In time, you will learn to do this meditation automatically—even in a room full of noisy, argumentative people.

3 Meditation To Tap Into The Etheric Body

The purpose of your etheric body is to link your spirit body to your earthly body. This etheric body is made up of energy that is fueled by earthly emotions and mental attitudes that the lower self creates, and the spiritual love energy that the Higher Self creates in a passionate response to the lower self's plea for help. This body is highly sensitive to its environmental surroundings and uses this as a built-in safety device to ensure survival. The more afraid you are, the more this body will try to escape any given situation. This meditation will assist you to face and eliminate your fears.

Knowing your own energies means careful study of the etheric body in different emotional, physical and mental stages. Meditation should be carried out in a detached manner with an understanding that its practice will result in a bonding of mind and emotions, resulting in peace. Test yourself when you are emotionally very low or highly elated.

- Say a prayer of protection, then complete the basic meditation and allow yourself to breathe slowly and deeply.

- Allow yourself to attune to your seven major chakras, which are rooted in your spine and, when expanded, blossom outward like a flower unfurling its petals. Begin by feeling the Root Chakra around the base of the spine. Visualize a tiny hole expanding outward to four to five inches in diameter. Breathe deeply several times and feel this expansion taking place around your genitals.

- Next, turn your attention to your Solar Plexus Chakra ,which lies at your abdomen, and again visualize a tiny hole expanding to six to seven inches in diameter. Breathe deeply, feeling this expansion taking place.

- Now, pay attention to your Heart Chakra, which lies over your chest, and visualize a small hole opening up to the size of a human heart. Breathe deeply and feel your chest expanding. By now, you will feel very relaxed and your breathing will begin to slow down, with longer inhalations and exhalations.

- Next, become aware of your Throat Chakra. Visualize a pinprick of a hole dilating to approximately two inches in diameter. Allow yourself to feel it opening. If you feel a need to swallow, do this until the need is gone.

- Now, direct your attention to your Third Eye Chakra. Give yourself mental permission to open it and visualize a larger-than-life eyelid opening to reveal an iris. Breathe deeply and feel the brow expanding.

- The Crown Chakra, which is always open, will now begin to expand. To aid this expansion, visualize a Chinese fan opening. See it revolving over your head. Allow yourself to feel the halo that exists around your head.

- Now, concentrate on the Spleen Chakra. See a small hole expanding to four inches in diameter and give yourself a mental command to balance the energy flowing through your body. Visualize a meter with a range of 0 to 100. Watch the needle center on 50. As you do this, allow yourself to feel your energies balancing within your body. Breathe deeply and know that you are ready now to begin receiving true wisdom from your superconscious and the spirit world.

- Breathe deeply and know that you can attune to any of your five bodies while in this deep state of meditation. Continue to breathe deeply as you accept this understanding.

- Allow your mind to focus on your etheric body. Begin to feel it with your mind as you normally do with your physical body. Breathe deeply and attune to how it feels. At first you will feel numb and then you will begin to sense that this body feels electrical. Accept this and breathe deeply.

- Understand that you are feeling your form of light and sound as an electrical current. Allow yourself to feel various kinds of prickling sensations and focus on the places that seem most intense. Notice how this area pulsates and tingles. Know that you are in the process of unblocking a fear.

- Allow the sensations you feel to build until you begin to hear whistling, whirling noises and to see colors in different hues pulsating toward and away from you. Accept that you are now releasing your fear.
- Lie still and enjoy these sensations. If there is some level of fear present that you do not wish to release, you will automatically bring yourself back to waking consciousness.
- Listen to yourself. Notice how amazingly indifferent you are to what you hear coming from your sleeping self, while at the same time you are acutely interested in what you feel and see both within yourself and in your immediate surroundings.
- Accept yourself as the observer and allow yourself to attune to any emanations that may arise. Watch as feelings of general emotions and irrational thoughts pass through and away from you. In this state, a great deal of tension, fear and hate can be released.
- When you have had enough, bring your attention back to God and His healing white light. Visualize the light as His healing hand caressing your body, gently revitalizing it, until you become aware once more of your physical body.
- When you feel ready, visualize all the Chakras closing by reversing the process one by one, starting with the Root Chakra as before and leaving the Crown Chakra partially open. Breathe deeply between the closing of each chakra.
- As before, close your Spleen Chakra last and visualize a meter with a dial ranging from 0 to 100. Watch the needle move to the halfway point and give yourself an order to balance your energies within the five bodies.
- Wait until you feel your normal bodily functions returning, then turn on your side and contemplate everything you have experienced. You may write everything down for your own records.

Note: At no time should you give way to fear. If fear does manifest while in meditation, challenge the conscious mind to experience something—it will find the spirit of adventure to continue.

4 Meditation To Tap Into The Spirit Body

Your spirit body is full of light and peace. Tapping into this body enables you to bring inner awareness forward to a conscious level, where you can then apply it to your everyday experiences. You will awaken to new ways to achieve a fuller life.

- Relax on your bed and complete the basic meditation.
- Say a prayer of protection. Visualize the Crown Chakra opening. When it is fully dilated, breathe deeply.
- Visualize the Third Eye Chakra opening and give it permission to see. Breathe deeply.
- Visualize the Heart Chakra as it opens. Begin breathing in long, slow breaths. When the Heart Chakra is open, allow yourself to attune to the feeling of God's love and accept the beautiful sensation of well-being as it flows through you.
- Visualize your Solar Plexus Chakra opening and feel at ease. Breathe deeply several times; let yourself sink into the bed.
- Visualize your Root Chakra opening and allow yourself to know that you will be releasing energy from this chakra. Breathe deeply.

- Finally visualize the Spleen Chakra opening. Balance them if necessary by adjusting the scales accordingly. Breathe slowly and deeply, feeling how relaxed and still you are.
- Now begin to feel the centers of the palms of your hands and soles of your feet. Allow these Minor Chakras to open, by visualizing tiny rings and watching them expand a little. Breathe deeply.
- Gently give yourself permission to raise your vibration and consciousness into the spirit body. Watch your body as you move quickly through the tingling and sounds of the etheric body and then into the spirit body.
- Notice if you feel you are laying in a different position or that some part of you feels thinner or fatter. Accept that this is normal and make a mental note of how you sense this body. It will appear to be perfect. Lay there and enjoy this new experience. Breathe deeply.
- Now invite the Creator's energy into your being. Wait patiently and allow yourself to feel His contact and upliftment. (There will be no mistaking your feelings from this experience. They will be very special to you.) Bathe in the love you feel and continue to breathe slowly and deeply.
- Now give permission for your guides to link with you and wait to see what happens. (You may merely see faces and familiar or unfamiliar places. You may feel you are becoming someone else by sharing in the Oneness.) Whatever happens, allow yourself to explore with your spirit guides. You will receive new insights. Enjoy them.
- When you have had enough, you will automatically return to the divine light. Bathe in this light and accept the healing offered to you. Allow yourself to become aware of a gentle sensation of falling backward. Drift with it until you become aware of your physical body.

- Take as long as necessary to close your Major and Minor Chakras and bring yourself back to waking consciousness.
- Contemplate everything you have experienced and write it down before it slips your mind. The act of writing allows the conscious mind to hold on to the memory of this experience and incorporate it into your everyday life.

Note: By focusing on the opening of the Crown Chakra first, you will have allowed yourself to leave earthly consciousness and to communicate with the spirit world, unhindered by the lower self. This meditation can be done many times a month, year in and year out. You will never tire of communicating with your spirit guides or of dealing with what, until now, has been the unknown.

5 MEDITATION TO TAP INTO THE HIGHER-MIND BODY

Obtaining contact with your Higher-Mind Body is not an easy task and may even seem impossible to some, at first. Keep trying the meditation periodically. When you succeed, you will find yourself full of wisdom far beyond your wildest fantasies. That wisdom may well be forgotten on a conscious level after you wake up, but on a subliminal level it will be remembered. Eventually, it will filter into your conscious self. It is important to practice this meditation without expectations and with a tremendous sense of trust in yourself.

- Complete the basic meditation. Breathe deeply and allow yourself to surrender to God and the trust that you have for Him and yourself.

- Open all your Major and Minor Chakras, beginning first with the Crown Chakra and ending with the balancing of the Spleen Chakra.
- Attune to your etheric body and allow yourself to feel this body and heal any parts that need restoring. Breathe deeply and relax further.
- Attune to your spirit body and allow yourself to feel this body. Let yourself enjoy contact with your spirit guides and ask them to assist you to touch your Higher Mind Body. Breathe deeply and allow them to lead you.
- Attune once again to God's love and surrender to his divine wisdom, allowing your vibration once again to be lifted. As you feel yourself being lifted, reach out to your Higher-Mind Body by telling yourself that you wish to be in a clear state of thought.
- Allow yourself to know that your conscious, subconscious and deep subconscious are becoming one. Watch your body grow numb and your emotions fade as you find your thoughts becoming clearer and clearer.
- Allow yourself to explore many concepts not previously conceived on a conscious level. Stay in this state as long as you like. (You will find you have no consciousness of the body; only an ever-evolving mind of wisdom.)
- When you have had enough, your awareness will return naturally to your spirit body, down through the etheric body and into your physical body. Breathe deeply and recall what you have learned from your Higher-Mind Body. Don't be discouraged if you don't remember a lot, as much of your experience will be unavailable to the conscious mind, though it is retained in the subconscious and deep subconscious.
- Visualize the light of God surrounding you as it replenishes and rebalances the body. Breathe deeply several times.

- Close all your Major and Minor Chakras, beginning with the Crown Chakra and ending with the balancing and closing of the Spleen Chakra. Move when ready and write everything down for your records.

6 Meditation For Channeling

Channeling is an activity that many wish to do but often find difficult to accomplish. The first step in becoming a channel medium involves complete mastery of the preceding meditations in this book. You should practice these meditations until you have learned to still the mind, discipline the body and express unconditional love in surrender. Once you can sit without fidgeting, with no thoughts beyond just being, your guides, who have been waiting patiently, will come close and share bodily sensations.

- Find a comfortable hard chair and sit in it with your back well supported. Keep your legs slightly apart, and bent comfortably at the knees, so that your feet are placed equally apart a little in front of the chair. Loosen any tight clothing.
- Say your own personal prayer of protection, asking for lost spirits and elementals to be uplifted and for negative thought forms and emotional expressions to be removed from you. Relax and breathe deeply several times.
- Envision the light of God flowing down from the heavens over and inside your head and body, washing all stress into the ground where Mother Nature uses it to rejuvenate the earth itself.

- Open your Major Chakras by visualizing them as previously described in this book, beginning with the Crown Chakra and working down to the Root. Lastly, open the Spleen and balance yourself. Open your hand and foot Minor Chakras. Breathe deeply.
- Ask your spirit guides to come close and touch you. At the same time, give yourself permission to feel them. Breathe deeply.
- Allow your breathing to deepen. Wait. Observe any body changes, such as feeling bigger, taller, smaller, fatter. Notice the emanations of hot and cold, shivers and chills that run through your spine, hands and feet. This is normal. Remain still and allow the feelings to become familiar. Continue to take slow, deep breaths.
- Give permission to your guides to enter your body and share it with you. Wait, and prepare for your breathing patterns to change.
- As the guide(s) enter, the feelings of bodily change will grow stronger. Note your breathing pattern as it begins to change. Let it happen. Receive healing from your spirit guides at this time.
- As you surrender your breathing to your spirit guides' control, cast all nervous thought forms and questions from your mind. Tell yourself everything feels fine. Sit and just be. Any self-made fears will disappear. (If they persist, then stop the meditation. You are not ready to continue. Close all chakras and bathe in white light.)
- All being well, allow yourself to feel a true sense of contentment flowing from your spirit guides into you. Be receptive now to your spirit guides' mind, allowing yourself to see and listen to their thoughts as they flow into your mind.
- Refrain from asking questions at this time. (At this point, your

conscious mind may try to interrupt. Override it.) Instead, when you are ready, speak aloud whatever words you may hear inside your head. Note how your breathing patterns continue to change as you move deeper and deeper into trance.

- Prepare yourself to receive physical feelings of slow movement when your spirit guides gently use their will to move your body. Cast out any fear that you may have of surrendering your body to your guides. Note your breathing patterns and slip deeper into trance. Accept that you are unable to move your body yourself—that you are asleep. Give yourself and your guide permission for movement to take place, then sit and wait.

- Watch your head and hands as they move first. Know that these are the easiest to move. Allow your conscious mind to absorb the mixed sensations that occur. Acknowledge how interesting it is to feel someone else moving your body. Remind your conscious mind that it is not in control and that it should not interfere. Do not allow your consicous mind to exaggerate the movement.

- Reach out to your spirit guide and surrender further.

- Allow your breathing to deepen as your spirit guides take greater control. Remind yourself that this is what you've waited for.

- As you flow into Oneness, your conscious mind will lose control. Accept that your Spirit Mind is functioning. If you desire to leave the body at this point, your spirit guides will help you do so by giving you a picture to center on. Let your being flow into the picture and go where it leads you. If you decide to stay in the body, you will begin to sense yourself in a new position on your seat, i.e. a little higher, or a little further forward or to the right or left, or further back. This is a clear indication that you have moved over in the body to make room for your spirit guide to literally share your body. Note your breathing patterns and surrender your energy even more to the will of your spirit guides.

- As your guide takes greater control, watch as your body begins to function without your control. Notice how your jaw and tongue move as your spirit guide prepares to speak through you. (You may make weird sounds.) Allow your guide to control your body. Let it continue and observe.
- When you are relaxed and in harmony, accept the words that begin to flow through your unified mind and out of your mouth. Do not monitor what you say. Just flow in communication. (These first words are usually messages for you. It is good to have someone present to record these words.)
- When you have both had enough, accept that your spirit guide will gently withdraw, returning control of your body to you. Watch as this happens; note your breathing patterns return to normal. Recognize that you are sleepy. Breathe gently.
- Visualize yourself closing your chakras from the Root upward, leaving the Crown open. Breathe deeply and send any excess energy you may feel into the ground through your foot chakras. Check that you feel normal.
- Visualize your Spleen Chakra and give the order to balance if you feel ill at ease. Bathe in the white light of God's love and congratulate yourself on a good meditation.
- Visualize closing your hand and foot chakras when you feel normal. Pull in the Crown Chakra and relax.
- Awaken, feeling refreshed. Write down your experiences.

DO'S AND DON'TS OF CHANNELLING

Don't Channel

– If there is any form of negativity present

– If you are ill

– If you feel lost spirits or elementals present

– If you are tired

– If you are afraid or unsure

– For others under pressure by demand

– To gain attention or respect from others

Do Channel

– If you are in the mood and sense your guides around

– If you are seeking guidance in a serene atmosphere

– To help others (but not at your own expense)

– For enlightenment and soul bonding

– In the presence of a teacher or spiritual person who can protect you and consciously guide you

Note: It takes time and practice to become an accomplished channel. Don't be disappointed when nothing happens. It merely means you are not quite ready, but know that you will still get a great deal out of the meditation, including healing.

7 MEDITATION FOR CONSCIOUS CHANNELING

Many people wish to channel but object to surrendering their body to spirit. If you are uncomfortable with such a process of surrender, then the following meditation will assist you to become a conscious channel only. (Place a tape recorder by your side, set it to record, and pause.)

• Find a comfortable hard chair and sit in it with your back well supported. Keep your legs slightly apart, and bent comfortably at the knees, so that your feet are placed equally apart a little in front of the chair. Loosen any tight clothing.

- Say your own personal prayer of protection, asking for lost spirits and elementals to be uplifted and for negative thought forms and emotional expression to be removed from you. Relax and breathe deeply several times.
- Envision the light of God flowing down from the heavens over and inside your head and body, washing all stress away.
- Open your Major Chakras by visualizing them expanding, beginning with the Crown Chakra and working down to the Root. Lastly, open the Spleen Chakra and breathe deeply as you sense yourself balancing your energies. Open your hand and foot Minor Chakras. Breathe deeply. Release the pause button on your tape recorder.
- Breathe deeply. Ask your spirit guides to begin giving you words to repeat out loud. Allow yourself to begin to develop a telepathic link.
- Breathe slowly and deeply as you hear the words and then repeat them. (Do not think about what you are saying.)
- Continue to breathe deeply and ask your spirit guides to give you sentences. Allow the sentences to form and say them aloud.
- Notice how sentences begin to flow from you. Continue to breathe deeply when necessary until communication ceases.
- Now, close your chakras and end your meditation by visualizing your chakras reducing to small pinholes. Breathe slowly and sense yourself returning to normal consciousness.
- Listen to your recording and allow yourself to absorb what has been said.

Note: At first, much of what you say will be garbled, as the words from your own mind mingle with the words from spirit. As you become more adept, a pattern of words will flow. With practice, you will notice how the words used by your spirit guides are expressed differently from your normal self. This will prove to you that you are not acting something out.

8 Meditation For Channeling Music

You may be musically inclined but feel uninspired. Your talent could be suppressed. By doing this meditation, you can share yourself with your spirit guides and produce some interesting work.

- Select a time in the future when you know you will be alone.
- On that day, prepare your mind several hours beforehand by contemplating your creativity and that of your spirit guides.
- When ready, bring your instrument to your side or go to it, if it is large, and bless it with love. Gently caress your instrument and create a picture of yourself playing it. Allow yourself to feel yourself becoming one with it.
- Sit with your instrument and breathe deeply several times. Attune to your spirit guides and the Creator. Ask for help with your music and accept that you are talented.
- Visualize yourself opening your chakras from the Crown on down to the Base (Root) Chakra. Attune to a blue/white light that is descending upon you and accept the presence of your spirit guides. Move into an altered state of consciousness.
- Ask your spirit guides to play your instrument with you through an act of sharing minds and emotions as one. Breathe

slowly and deeply, caressing your instrument.

- As you sit there, allow your desire to grow. Continue to caress your instrument as your spirit guides share your body.
- Allow a spontaneous feeling to stimulate you to begin playing. Breathe deeply; let your fingers feel and explore as your spirit guides explore with you. Surrender control to your spirit guides' control and allow your breath to flow as your body relaxes. Feel the music flowing through you. Be the musician.
- Play the notes your hands desire to play. Move with the vibration of your playing. Allow any awkwardness to flow away. Feel the music emerging from your soul.
- Play until you and your spirit guides have had enough, then put your instrument down. Thank your spirit guides and promise to try again another time.
- Sense your spirit guides leaving and close your chakras through visualization. Wait until you feel normal again. Listen to what you have created without criticism.

9 Meditation For Channeling Writing

As a child, you had a great sense of imagination, full of ideas. The child within you may well be longing to write a short story, poetry or a novel. The following is step-by-step guidance to assist you to tap into that inner child.

- Find a quiet room to be alone. Have paper and pen ready.
- Say your prayer to God, asking for guidance and protection.

- Focus your mind on your spirit guides and ask them to come close and share with you. Breathe deeply several times.
- Visualize yourself opening your Major Chakras, beginning with your Crown. Continue to breathe deeply.
- Open your eyes, pick up the pen and hold it over the paper.
- Close your eyes and breathe deeply several times. Center your mind, while allowing your body simply to be.
- Begin by writing your thoughts down, no matter what they are. Write everything you think. (Do not stop to read or digest what you write.) Allow your thoughts to merge with your spirit guide's thoughts. Know that you will eventually write words from spirit.
- Breathe deeply and allow the momentum of your mind to increase. Become absorbed with what you are writing.
- When writing comes to an end, you will feel a lack of desire to write further. Read what you have written.
- If you have a question about what is written, ask it mentally. Breathe deeply and prepare to write the answer.
- Begin writing as before until the desire to cease writing flows over you.
- Thank your spirit guides for their help and remind them that you would like to write more in the future.
- Visualize yourself closing your chakras. Return to normal consciousness and store your writings away for reference.

Note: In the early days of practicing inspirational writing, much of what you write will be rubbish. This will teach you just how much your conscious mind rambles. Remember, the conscious mind does not like to be shown up and will soon correct itself. In time and with practice, your writings from spirit will become clear.

MEDITATION FOR CHANNELING ART 10

Becoming a psychic artist can be very rewarding. Developing this talent can stimulate you to draw spirit guides, friends and loved ones of your own and of other people as well as scenes from the spirit world. You don't need to be artistically trained, you just need a willingness to allow your innate talent to emerge and blend with those of your spirit guide. Together, you will create wonderful art. In the early days, your scribbles will often be meaningless or very shaky, to say the least. With practice, you will perfect a technique unique to yourself and your spirit guides.

- Allow yourself to indulge in the idea of producing great art. Do this over a period of several days.
- Attune each day to your spirit guides and ask for their help. Pick a day and time to begin practicing. Buy an art pad and pencils, paints, crayons, or other tools. (Children's school equipment is adequate to start with; you can upgrade your art tools later.)
- During these days, allow yourself to become familiar with your new equipment. Sit and handle the tools with love and care.
- On the day you have chosen to begin your new talent, do the basic meditation, then sit in a comfortable chair with your tools within easy reach.
- Begin by saying your own prayer of protection and ask for your spirit guides to come close.

- Breathe deeply and open your chakras, from the Crown to the Root, by visualizing a small white dot over each one, then expanding the dot.

- Breathe deeply and allow yourself to harmonize with your spirit guides. Let yourself feel their presence and enthusiasm. Cast away all negative ideas about your creativity.

- When the feeling to draw emerges, begin to lightly scribble. Let yourself sense your hand as separate from your body and give it the freedom to do anything on the paper. Breathe deeply and watch your hand as it moves. (You may not know what you are drawing.)

- As you watch, continue to breathe deeply and sense the artistic creativity of your spirit guides. Blend with them.

- Allow yourself to become absorbed in your artistic talent and see what you are drawing, enjoy and relax.

- Become inspired and if the desire to add color flows, then do so.

- Continue until you are finished. If there are any psychic messages from your spirit guide about the picture, write them down.

- Admire your work and thank your spirit guides for their help. Close your eyes and visualize your chakras, one at a time, and watch them close, by seeing large white circles over each one reducing to tiny dots again. Breathe deeply and return to normal consciousness.

- Keep this first drawing for reference. Your later attempts will improve as time goes on.

Note: Some psychic artists feel that their entire body has become the artist. Others find themselves drawing as though tracing an outline. Whichever happens, it will be done in a way that comes naturally to you.

MEDITATION TO OBSERVE THE AKASHIC RECORDS

11

The Akashic Records are the vibrational coding of the Holy Spirit. By tapping into this part of the Holy Spirit, one can find out about anything that has ever been created by God. You may wish to discover more about yourself and those you know. You should, however, remember that it is only possible for you to obtain information that will help you and others. The following is a meditation that will help a developing psychic to tap into the Akashic Records.

- Find a comfortable place where you will not be disturbed and do the basic meditation. Breathe slowly and deeply and then open your Major Chakras by visualizing each chakra expanding from a tiny hole until it is fully dilated.
- Breathe deeply and ask your spirit guides to protect you and assist you to move your energy into the right vibration for reading the Akashic Records. Continue to breathe deeply and allow your spirit guides to lead you.
- Focus on the idea of ascending consciousness and give yourself permission to proceed.
- Breathe deeply several times and visualize a pink cloud by your side. Climb onto it and allow yourself to feel its movement as you sit there. Breathe deeply and allow yourself to become one with the cloud and feel yourself drifting forward or upward.
- Breathe deeply and focus on what you wish to see that is relative to yourself at this time, as you drift.

- Notice that the cloud is taking you toward a light. Enjoy yourself as you receive healing and move into your spirit consciousness.

- Breathe deeply and allow your spiritual eyes to focus on a scene. Observe it as it unfolds.

- Make mental notes and breathe deeply. Ask your spirit guides to assist you to see it again from another angle. Wait and observe the same scene. (There will be differences. You may do this as often as you wish until you have the full picture.)

- If you desire to see something different, breathe deeply and allow yourself to be on your pink cloud again. Feel it drifting once more until you see a new scene. Breathe deeply as you observe and check it again from other angles.

- When you have had enough, return your consciousness to your pink cloud and relax. Breathe slowly and deeply and remind yourself of your discoveries.

- When you are ready, command your pink cloud to return. Breathe slowly. Feel yourself withdrawing.

- Watch as your breathing returns to normal and you become aware of your body. Keeping your eyes shut, relax and contemplate all that you have seen. Go over it until your conscious mind has accepted what has been revealed.

- Visualize your Major Chakras closing. Pull in your muscles over each chakra. Breathe slowly as you do this. Move as in awakening. Continue to recall all you have seen.

- When you're ready, sit up and write everything down for your records.

Note: Attuning to the Akashic Records will give you insight into the enormity of the Oneness, where all things are known. This new awareness will change you on all levels—emotionally, mentally and physically—for the better.

Meditation To Become One With The Akashic Records

12

Practicing this meditation, quite simply, means erasing your personal history and allowing yourself to look with the eyes of God. If you are lucky enough to achieve this oneness, your outlook on a conscious level will be completely changed. Set a special time aside and prepare for this occasion in your own way.

- Play your favorite meditation music and relax in a comfortable chair. Let this life and its problems drift away from you.
- Breathe slowly and deeply and push away all your fears. Remind yourself that your fear will prevent you from touching and feeling the Oneness. Continue to breathe deeply.
- Reach out to God the Creator with a prayer and visualize his light descending from above to encompass you. Breathe deeply and absorb this healing light into your body and feel your deeper fears being washed away.
- Focus on your Major Chakras and visualize them expanding. Relax the muscles over each chakra.
- Breathe deeply and reach out to your spirit guides. Ask them to assist you on your journey. Sense them becoming one with you. Continue to breathe slowly and deeply.
- Give yourself permission to ascend into the Oneness.
- Visualize a stairway that appears to be endless and begin to climb it. Be patient and loving with yourself as you climb. Breathe deeply and know that you will move through your other bodies as you ascend.

- Allow yourself to feel bodily changes as you move through your physical, etheric, spirit and mind bodies. Relax more and more as each change occurs. Continue breathing slowly.
- Watch yourself as you grow mentally and emotionally indifferent to yourself. Accept this. Breathe deeply. Acknowledge that God's thoughts and emotions are unconditional. Let them flow into you.
- Breathe deeply. Notice that the stairway is dissolving and you are beginning to feel your presence in all things. Let your mind reveal many strange and unusual things. Enjoy this unveiling.
- Breathe deeply and let your feelings of love grow deeper and deeper.
- Allow these deep feelings to flow and join with anything you sense or see. Give up control and surrender.
- Breathe deeply and know that quite suddenly you will be in the Oneness. Allow this very individual and personal experience to occur. Let your joy be immense. Know that your knowledge is great yet undefined. Watch as the Akashic Records unfold with you as the center. Allow yourself to feel that you have come home. Enjoy for as long as it lasts. (Brief as it is, it will seem like an eternity.)
- As you withdraw, breathe deeply and recognize any sense of loss that you feel is natural. Prepare to descend in vibration. Look for the stairway.
- Breathe slowly and begin to climb down. Do not rush. Slowly descend the stairs. Feel yourself drifting back through your four bodies until you are conscious of where you are sitting.
- Breathe deeply and mentally check your energy flow. If you feel too light or dizzy, visualize yourself making a ball with this excess energy and tossing it towards a loved one as a form of healing.

- Breathe deeply again and allow yourself to relax. Thank your spirit guides for helping you and physically close your chakras, pulling the muscles in and visualizing the large discs returning to small pinholes over each one.
- Visualize the Spleen Chakra as the scales of justice. Place weights in the pans and make them level. Know that this visualization will harmonize the changes in you. Breathe deeply and arouse yourself slowly. Immediately write your experiences down.

Note: Ninety percent of what you will have experienced will be lost from the conscious mind. Remember that this information will seep down through your spirit mind into consciousness with time. This meditation should only be attempted once or twice a year.

Meditation To Erase Personal History By Surrender 13

If it has been impossible for you to let go of controlling habits and you wish to let go of this conditioning, this meditation will help you to recreate a mindset that is strong and flexible. Practicing this meditation will affect your daily life immediately. People, places and things will be less distracting or worrisome. You will find that the more you let go, the calmer and easier life becomes.

- Sit in a relaxed position in a comfortable chair.
- Breathe deeply and let go of the stress you carry and say a prayer of protection.
- Visualize your chakras and feel the muscles over each one.

Beginning with the Root Chakra, watch each one opening and expanding. Let the muscles relax at the same time. Breathe slowly and deeply several times and open the foot and hand mini-chakras in the same way. Relax and breathe deeper.

- Allow yourself to feel the presence of your guides and ask for their help. Breathe deeply and feel yourself harmonizing with them.
- In your mind's eye, select one of your many treasures to focus on, such as a favorite piece of jewelry.
- See it hanging in front of you. Fondle it in your mind and recall why you like it so much. Breathe deeply.
- Observe your reasons for keeping it and begin to contemplate the idea of giving it away.
- Observe the emotions that arise when you think of giving it away. Breathe deeply and watch how your body tenses.
- Tell yourself you do not need to keep it, no matter what reasons your mind invents for continued possession.
- Breathe slowly and deeply and give yourself permission to lose control.
- Now create in your mind a stranger. Give the treasure to that person.
- Observe your reactions as you give it away.
- Watch the stranger and see what the stranger does with the treasure. Breathe deeply and allow yourself to know that these pictures are the manifestation of fears based on past experiences, such as the fear that they might drop it, misuse it or give it away.
- Let yourself realize that these reactions are possessive and controlling. Breathe deeply and give yourself permission to override these pictures.

- Once again, visualize this stranger misusing your treasured belonging. Breathe deeply and allow yourself to be indifferent to it. Observe this emotion.
- Ask your spirit guides to help you release your hold on this item. Watch symbolic or literal pictures that manifest. Recognize the help that you are receiving and promise yourself to practice releasing in this way in the future. Breathe deeply and allow yourself to feel all tension that has been held in your body as a reminder to surrender control. Continue to breathe slowly and relax.
- Visualize the closing of your Major and Minor Chakras. Watch each one shrink to a pinhole, pulling the muscles in. Breathe slowly and thank your spirit guides and God for their assistance.
- Move slowly and write your discoveries down immediately.

Note: This meditation can be practiced often with many different items. When you feel ready, do this also with your loved ones. Give them to someone else. In the meditation, see them leaving you—watch your emotions, live your fears, then give yourself permission to release them. Watch them go and give them your blessings as they leave. Wait for the feeling of neutrality to arise and then finish the meditation.

Meditation To Surrender Control To Your Spirit Will 14

Do this meditation after the previous one has become easy and your life has become more simple. Acting upon your spirit will is acting out the will of God in oneness consciousness. With practice, your conscious will of resistance will surrender, allowing you to become more spontaneous and have a complete awareness of everything you do.

- Sit in a relaxed position in a comfortable chair.
- Breathe deeply and let go of the stress you carry and say a prayer asking for protection and healing.
- Visualize your chakras and feel the muscles over each one. Beginning with the Root Chakra, watch each one opening by observing it expand from a pinhole to a solid large disc. Let the muscles relax at the same time. Breathe slowly and deeply several times and open the feet and hand chakras in the same way. Relax and breathe deeper.
- Mentally tell yourself that you are lost. Breathe deeply and look around. Know that there is no one to come to your rescue.
- Breathe deeper and observe emotions arising. Allow yourself to face them by letting them climax. Cry if necessary.
- Breathe deeply and give yourself permission to be strong for yourself. Continue to breathe deeply. You will begin to see the uselessness of your fears.
- Visualize yourself as a small child and allow yourself to love this child. Pick the child up and hold it to you. Tell your child self what it needs to hear that will comfort it.
- As the child in your arms becomes comforted, allow it to sink into your body. Breathe deeply and feel the child within. Relax and breathe slowly.
- Allow yourself to visualize a stranger who is your spirit guide and allow him/her to give advice to both the adult and child parts of you. See yourself as found. Breathe deeply.
- Visualize the closing of your Major Chakras by watching each one shrink to a pinhole, pulling the muscles in at the

same time. Breathe slowly and thank your spirit guides and God for their assistance.

- Release any excess energy into the ground by visualizing it flowing as water from the soles of your feet and hands. Close these Minor Chakras by contracting the muscles and feeling them shut.
- Move slowly and write down your discoveries about yourself immediately.

Meditation For Receiving 15

Many people are able to give to others easily but find it very difficult to receive anything for themselves. This meditation will help you to build up your levels of self-esteem and allow you to accept everything that is vicariously given to you from God, the Creator. This meditation can be practiced daily.

- Relax in a comfortable chair. Play some meditation music and gently allow yourself to focus on receiving.
- Say your own special prayer and ask your spirit guides to come and share with you. Breathe deeply and trust them to bless you and keep you safe.
- Visualize the Creator as a cloud of white light descending toward you. Watch it as the cloud drifts onto your head. Feel the Crown Chakra opening. Let your face relax, and sense this cloud moving down your body, opening each chakra as it passes. Sense how relaxed you feel. Allow yourself to feel

open and ready to receive. Breathe deeply several times.

- Visualize yourself walking along a pathway with your spirit guide leading you.
- Breathe deeply and let your spirit guides take you to a place of their choice.
- Breathe slowly and deeply as you survey the scene. Ask them to give you something. Watch what is given and interpret its symbolic meaning. If you cannot, ask for its meaning.
- Breathe deeply and attune to any feelings that may arise as a result of this gift and your new understanding. Breathe slowly and feel this emotion swelling up in your heart. Express it aloud.
- Breathe and relax. As you calm down, make a firm promise to allow yourself to receive again and again.
- Now begin to breathe deeply and allow a feeling of utter joy to fill your entire being as you receive unconditional love from God. Sit and savor this moment.
- Let your spirit guides gently lead you back to an awareness of your physical body. Breathe slowly and evenly.
- Thank your spirit guides for the present you have received and allow them to close your Major and Minor Chakras for you. When you feel they are closed, move your body gently and when ready, stretch.
- Keep records of all your reactions to the meditation for appraisal at a later date.

Note: With practice, the ability to receive will grow easier. It will also become easier to receive in everyday life, which also makes giving easier.

MEDITATION TO ACCEPT GOD'S WILL AS PERSONAL WILL

16

The following meditation will assist you to attune to the Creator's desires, enabling you to surrender and discover that His will is your will, ultimately leading to total contentment physically, emotionally and mentally.

- Find a quiet place, such as a park, a quiet garden, a mountaintop, or ocean shore.
- Sit and emotionally attune to your surroundings. Breathe deeply for a while. Allow yourself to release all worries and stress.
- Sit in a crosslegged position with your back erect. Breathe deeply and find the central balance of your body, so that there is no effort in sitting.
- Continue to breathe deeply and say your own personal prayer asking for enlightenment and protection.
- Visualize your Major Chakras expanding, one by one, leaving the Spleen Chakra for last. As you focus on the Spleen Chakra, visualize a meter from one to 100 and watch the needle move to 50. Breathe deeply and open your foot and hand chakras.
- Breathe deeply and as you exhale become aware of the mini-chakras that lie over your acupressure points. Know that they are opening by merely surrendering to the flow of your energies. Allow yourself to twitch as this happens.
- Breathe deeply and allow yourself to receive love from the God-force. Notice how uplifted you feel.

- Continue to breathe deeply and mentally ask how you may serve in the best way for God and yourself. Wait patiently. Accept that you may wait a long time as you are healed and tested with patience and endurance of body, mind and spirit.

- Accept that as you wait, your body may become painful as you sit in this fixed upright position. Breathe deeply and refrain from moving. Accept that you are moving through your experience of the pains of the world.

- Continue to breathe deeply and allow yourself to move into a true altered state of consciousness in which you realize you feel and know God's words within yourself. Allow your spirit guides to communicate and bond with you. Notice how you all appear to be present together in a semi-physical, spiritual form. Recognize that you are now in your spirit body consciousness.

- Breathe deeply and listen to your spirit guides as they lead and counsel you towards the Oneness. Listen to the questions your spirit guides ask. Observe your Higher Self responses and know that these questions are assisting you to reveal more about yourself to your Lower Self.

- Breathe deeply and ask for physical directions that will lead you into a better style of living, where you can express yourself fully. Breathe deeply and cast out any doubt from yourself by acknowledging this truth. (Your spirit guides know you have doubts. If your will is God's will, you will want to go without fear or question.) Breathe deeply and mentally promise to follow these directions.

- Continue to breathe deeply and recognize that the way will be shown to you as you follow these directions. Promise yourself that you will not fantasize and misdirect yourself. Accept that your emotions will guide you in a positive way. Breathe deeply and feel your joy in accepting direction from the Oneness.

- Allow God's love to flow through you, washing away any fears or uncertainties that you have and accept new feelings of security that replace them.
- Breathe deeply and let your spirit guides separate from you when this meditation is finished.
- Visualize your Major Chakras closing one by one. Breathe deeply and visualize your Spleen Chakra as a meter once more. Continue to breathe slowly and accept that you are now one with your spirit guides and have no need to thank them as you are now equal to them. Focus your mind on this understanding and allow yourself to consciously be receptive to them.
- Continue to breathe slowly as you close your Minor Chakras and then gently move until you are in a relaxed position.
- Contemplate your experience, then write down all that occurred for future reference.

Note: Often, this type of meditation will take several hours, though you will be totally unaware of time. Remember, all that was communicated will not necessarily occur immediately. There is a correct time and place for everything.

MEDITATION FOR TRANSCENDENTAL AWARENESS 17

If you desire to reach higher levels of awareness where you can begin to understand the whole of creation and talk to great spiritual beings, such as Jesus and Buddha, this meditation will take you there, but you must have reached a point in your life where you are ready to surrender in grace to the will of the Creator. This meditation is designed to assist you to move into a transcendental state where all aspects of life can be contemplated in the way of Oneness.

- Relax, lying prone on a bed or the floor in loose clothing.
- Breathe deeply and say your personal prayer of protection and attunement to God's love.
- Visualize the light of God flowing through your body as it moves from your head to your toes.
- Breathe deeply and allow your physical body to relax as all stress is washed away into the ground where Mother Nature uses it to rejuvenate the earth itself.
- Breathe deeply and visualize yourself opening all seven Major Chakras and then the Minor Chakras. Continue to breathe deeply as you attune to the collective soul consciousness, which includes your higher self and your spirit guides.
- Allow your breathing pattern to become longer and deeper between each inhalation and attune to your etheric body. Allow the energy to build; you will tingle and quiver all over as it builds. Exhale and allow your breath to sweep any stress held in the body through your feet chakras into the ground.
- Now allow yourself to attune to your spirit body. As you inhale deeply, sense any changes in body temperature and acknowledge your spirit body. Exhale any stress held in this body through the feet chakras as before. Continue to breathe slowly and deeply.
- Now, gently attune to your mental body and tell your lower self that you wish to be in a clear state of thought. Breathe slowly and deeply several times, and sense your conscious, subconscious and deep subconscious minds becoming one.
- Allow your breathing pattern to find a balance and know that

your four bodies are uniting as one body. Breathe deeply and let go as you sense a feeling of numbness manifesting itself.

- Allow yourself to drift as you explore many new concepts. Stay as long as you like in this space.
- When you have had enough, allow yourself to automatically drift back into awareness of your spirit body, then the etheric, and finally the physical body.
- Breathe slowly and relax as you try to recall the essence of things contemplated (much of what you have discovered will be lost on a conscious level).
- Close all your Major Chakras from Crown to Root by contracting the muscles over each one. Breathe slowly and sense how you feel. If you feel light-headed, send this excess energy out through the hand chakras to a loved one as healing for them. Then visualize your minor chakras closing.
- Move slowly when ready. Write down your experiences for future reference.

Note: This meditation should be done on a day when you will not be disturbed by anyone or anything for at least 48 hours, during which time you will go through many emotional and mental changes. A quiet weekend spent alone would be ideal.

MEDITATION FOR SELF-HEALING 18

If you suffer from an injury or minor ailment, this meditation will help you to heal. It helps you draw energy from God to revitalize the affected area and induce the beginnings of a cure. If this meditation has no effect, then you must go back and look for the cause of the illness. You can accomplish this by doing a meditation on the etheric body to discover what emotional or mental anguish has caused the complaint. This is especially useful in cases of serious illness or disease such as cancer.

- Allow yourself to relax. Breathe deeply and say a prayer of your choosing that assists you to become aware of God's presence and your oneness with Him and the universe.
- Breathe deeply and focus your mind on the area to be healed. Sense its condition and let yourself visualize an exaggerated picture of its appearance. (For example, you may sense a swelling as much as ten times bigger than it is or an open wound seemingly more serious than it really is.)
- Continue to breathe slowly and mentally explore the area to be healed. If you perceive it as something strange, such as a lump of coal, then flow with your concept and see how you can shape it into something that delights your eye and your emotions. Watch as it turns into something beautiful.
- If your thoughts remain rooted in realism, then visualize your body as a solid white form, and place a dark patch on the place to be healed. Now, breathe deeply and look for areas of red—this is where you are carrying excess energy. Breathe deeply. In your mind's eye, begin to move this excess energy toward the area needing healing by massaging this picture of energy, rather like squeezing a tube of toothpaste.
- Breathe deeply and watch this energy arrive at the designated spot. Observe this red energy mixing with your dark patch. Watch as the this dark patch changes colors until it becomes white like the rest of the form.
- Breathe deeply and allow yourself to fall asleep, so that rejuvenation can take place on a physical level.

MEDITATION FOR DIVINE HEALING

19

The following meditation attunes you to receive divine healing. It should be done early in the morning and last thing at night—these are the times when one is in harmony with the spirit consciousness (the deep subconscious).

- Play some meditation music if possible. Lie on your back in bed with the covers pulled up to your chin. (If you are sleeping with a partner, ensure freedom from being disturbed by telling him or her what you are going to do.)
- Align your body so that you feel square and straight, hands resting loosely beside you. Breathe deeply and relax.
- Close your eyes. Sense your body and its weight. If it feels uneven, move until your weight feels equal all over.
- Sense your sick body's position in bed. Breathe deeply. Say your own personal prayer, asking God for healing.
- Recognize your tension by feeling the aches and pains of your body. Acknowledge the stress you feel. Breathe deeply and surrender this stress and tension to God.
- Envision God's white light as a giant hand above your head. Watch as it radiates an electric blue ray over you, saturating your entire being and healing you on all levels.
- Watch your physical body relax as you begin to breathe slowly and deeply. Watch the aches and pains leave you.
- Continue to breathe deeply and watch this electric blue ray turn golden and enter the area to be healed. Surrender to the

will of God and his pleasure in healing you.

- See the diseased matter being washed out through the surface of your body, where it disintegrates and turns to gas. Breathe deeply and allow yourself to listen to the music that is playing.
- Continue to breathe deeply and allow your mind to observe the entire healing process that takes place. Know that when it is completed, you will clearly see an improvement or cure
- Now that the healing process is completed, allow yourself the luxury of being in visual contemplation of a safe haven, where you are relaxing. Breathe slowly and allow yourself to drift into sleep with the conscious knowledge that this healing work will continue throughout the night.

Note: For the morning meditation, you may shorten the relaxation procedure, as your body is already relaxed. Remember to acknowledge God in your activities. Treat yourself with love following this kind of healing. Remember, it takes time to undo past wrongs which have resulted in fear and disease, so be patient.

20 Meditation For Corrective Healing

If you wish to do a more concentrated healing meditation, it is important to study the anatomical form, providing a conscious awareness of where everything is located in the body. This enables you to experience intense healing while in deep meditation.

- Relax and complete the basic meditation.
- Breathe deeply and visualize your body as though you are

observing it as someone else's body, but feel it from within. Attune yourself to your working knowledge of your body and its functions.

- Visualize God's healing energy as electric blue light descending upon you.
- Open the Major and Minor Chakras. Breathe deeply.
- Attune yourself to your nervous system by visualizing a white physical form with strings all over it. Focus on God's light and watch it form a small ball, rolling along the strings as it makes its way down and around the body system, beginning at the head until you return to your starting point. Continue to breathe deeply.
- Attune yourself to your circulatory system in the same way, follow the healing light around this system, then return to your starting point.
- Attune yourself to the lymphatic system in the same manner and continue to breathe deeply.
- Attune yourself to your muscles from head to toe. Watch this healing ball of light move within each muscle. Continue breathing deeply.
- Attune yourself to each bone individually throughout the body, once more visualizing this ball of healing light in each one. Continue breathing deeply.
- Attune yourself to each vital organ (one at a time) and see within it. Look at its structure and see the healing ball of light cleansing and rebuilding where necessary. (Suggested order for concentration on the organs are: brain, eyes, lungs, heart, stomach-duodenum, liver, spleen, pancreas, kidneys, intestines, bowel, bladder, genitals.) Continue to breathe deeply.
- Attune yourself to your passages—esophagus, bronchial tubes and canals, sinuses—and see the white ball of light healing

them individually. Breathe deeply once more.

- Attune yourself to your glands—pituitary, thyroid, thalamus, pineal, inguinal, and sex organs and glands—and see the ball of healing white light dancing around them. Breathe deeply.

- Attune yourself to your ligaments and tendons where the healing light rebuilds and strengthens them. Breathe deeply.

- Attune yourself to the spaces between your organs and see the ball of white light healing these parts. Breathe deeply.

- Attune yourself to your head, nose, mouth, ears, pharynx and larynx. Visualize the white ball of light healing them. Breathe deeply.

- Attune your consciousness to any body parts you may have overlooked and send the ball of white light to heal them. Follow the white light to discover what you have forgotten. Breathe deeply.

- Attune yourself to your skin and watch the ball of white light expand to encompass your entire body. See how it glows. Breathe slowly and deeply.

- Lie still and feel the Oneness with God's energy surrounding you. Feel the healing you have received. Breathe slowly.

- When you are ready, close your chakras and allow yourself to awaken slowly into full consciousness. Thank God for his help and congratulate yourself on a job well done. Move slowly throughout the rest of the day to preserve the healing.

Note: This meditation will leave you with a truly wonderful sense of well-being and improvement. Do not make the mistake of rushing about. It takes many such meditations to complete an effective cure. Always treat yourself with care, as though you have just returned from a hospital and are convalescing.

Meditation For Self-Cleansing The Chakras

21

Torn or dirty chakras can lead to depression and a variety of discomforts which, if not repaired, can result in serious diseases. If you are unable to find a healer to work on cleansing your chakras, the following meditation will help you do it yourself.

- Complete the basic meditation, and say your personal prayer for protection and healing.
- Visualize God's healing white light above your head. Breathe deeply and watch as it descends to the top of your head and enters your Crown Chakra to open it wide.
- Breathe deeply. Ask yourself if this chakra is blocked or broken in some way. Wait for an image to be given to you which will show you clearly its state of being—for example, a circle without clearly defined edges.
- In your mind, repair it by defining how you think it should be. Spend time forming it until you can clearly visualize it as perfect. Breathe slowly and deeply and sense the healing work done.
- Now, feel the white light flowing down into your Third Eye Chakra. Breathe deeply and give yourself permission to see how it looks. Wait for a picture of an eye looking at you. Note its appearance. If it is shut, open it and look deeply into it for flaws. Whatever you see that is flawed or damaged, visualize it as you wish to see it. Repair it where necessary until it is clearly defined. Breathe deeply and acknowledge this healing.

- Attune yourself to the Throat Chakra. Visualize the white light moving into it. Once again, wait for the pictures that will show you its condition. If you are dissatisfied with any part of it, rebuild it until you have it to your liking. Breathe slowly and deeply. Acknowledge the healing work done on this chakra.

- Then watch the white light descend and enter your Heart Chakra. Observe the picture that arises and repair it where necessary. Breathe deeply and observe the white light as it cleanses this chakra and uplifts you emotionally.

- Breathe deeply and follow the white light into your Solar Plexus Chakra. Observe the picture that arises. It should look like a sieve. If it is torn, repair it by sewing in a new cover over the old one and know that they will bond together. Watch the white light cleanse and strengthen this chakra.

- Breathe deeply. When ready, watch the white light move down into the Root Chakra. Wait for the visual picture to appear and begin to rebuild it where necessary. Breathe deeply again and watch the white light cleanse this chakra.

- Now, notice how the Spleen Chakra has already absorbed the white light and is already in the process of healing. Wait for a visual picture of the state of this chakra to appear. You can assist its rejuvenation by watching the white light changing colors as it moves through the spectrum. Breathe slowly and deeply as each color appears.

- Now that you have repaired the chakras visually in the physical sense, it is time to return to each one and relate them individually to the other four bodies. Breathe deeply and allow yourself to drift into a higher state of awareness.

- First scan the Crown Chakra for any black blobs. If you find one, surround it with light. If you wish to know which body it lies in, simply ask yourself and feel the response from your Higher Self. If it remains visible with the light (still a dark blob), then begin to mentally change the light that surrounds it, running through the spectrum colors from red to purple until it disappears.

- Breathe deeply and know that you are attuning your Spleen Chakra to the Crown Chakra to create harmony.

- Once the Crown Chakra is clear, do the same with the other five Major Chakras, allowing each one to be tuned by the Spleen Chakra until all the blobs have disappeared. Breathe deeply through this part of the meditation. (If any blobs remain after persistent healing, then you must accept that there is something deep within you that needs to be brought into full consciousness. Do not try to do this now. Merely accept this understanding and continue to heal the other chakras.)

- Now that you have healed all the chakras to the best of your ability, visualize yourself closing them down to pinpricks, while pulling in the muscles over each one. Gently bring yourself back to full waking consciousness.

- Congratulate yourself on a job well done and thank the Creator and your spirit guides for assisting you to work with your Higher Self.

Note: Any blobs, otherwise known as blocks, that refused to be absorbed into the healing light can be worked on in meditation at a later date by meditating intensely on the body, bring pain and discomfort to the surface for observation and full understanding. This, of course, can only be done when you are ready to face yourself and erase this emotional fear, which may not necessarily come from this life, but rather from a previous one, particularly if the block lies in the spirit body.

22 Meditation For Astral Travel And Healing

Your motive for leaving your body may well be a selfish one on a conscious level. However, as soon as you achieve this state, you will find yourself drawn to others and will quite naturally begin to share yourself and heal those you meet. If you have a loved one who is sick, this meditation will assist you to focus your conscious mind towards assisting them to recover from a spiritual advantage point. This meditation may also be used for acquiring new knowledge from the spirit world and this world.

- First attune to your spirit guides and say a prayer asking for protection from all negative thoughts and fears that you may have.
- Lie on your back and make yourself comfortable. Allow your thoughts to drift away and begin to gently move into a positive state of mind. Breathe deeply several times until you find yourself totally relaxed.
- Now, think about the person you wish to heal. Recognize how much love you feel for them and how much you want to help them. Breathe slowly and deeply.
- Let yourself feel God's love in your heart, lifting your vibration towards Him.
- Take a deep breath and begin to open your Major Chakras by visualizing them open as you relax the muscles that lie over each one.
- Allow your consciousness to drift beyond your physical and

etheric bodies and gently begin to attune to the feeling of your spirit body. Begin now to breathe very slowly, with long deep breaths, as you feel this body.

- Now create a picture of your sick friend with your mind's eye. See your friend standing before you. Breathe deeply and allow yourself to feel all the unconditional love you have for this person.

- Now, in your mind's eye, take your friend's hand and prepare to leave your body. Breathe deeply and hold them tightly as you give yourself permission to leave your body and wait.

- Listen to yourself breathing as you sleep and hear the roaring noise around your ears as your spirit begins to leave. (If you find yourself spinning, you are afraid, so turn over and go into a deep sleep now. You will still leave your body and visit your friend and do what is necessary, but without recall).

- Assuming that you are consciously continuing with this meditation, begin to gently rise up out of bed either in a floating manner, or literally as you normally do, by sitting up and getting up. Now you are out of body. Spend a moment and feel how emotionally free you feel.

- Now, think about your sick friend and allow your desire to impel you to be by their side immediately. Your friend may be sleeping or out of body too.

- Become aware of your spirit guides. Ask for their assistance to heal your friend. Let your true self work with them to heal your friend. Recognize how skilled you are and make a mental note to allow your conscious mind to recall your work.

- Know that when you are finished, you will leave and either return to bed and sleep, or go on to other pressing activities from which you will return to your body later. Keep reminding your lower self that it can remember everything that you are doing.

- When you have journeyed enough, allow yourself to feel your spirit being pulled slowly backwards toward your physical body. Gently settle into it and become aware of being back in your bed.
- Become aware of your breathing patterns and gently remind your conscious mind about all the things you have done as you wait patiently for your body to wake up.
- As soon as you can move, put the light on and write down everything you can remember or recite it into a tape recorder. When you have finished, put out the light and lie once more on your back.
- Breathe slowly and rhythmically as you visualize each one of your Major Chakras closing. Remember to pull in the muscles over each one so that your conscious mind can rest easy.

Note: You may not feel like sleeping, so get up, have a beverage and then return to bed for normal sleeping. Despite the guidance given with the last part of this meditation you are not likely to recall your return, but will find yourself dreaming about a small part of what has occurred. This will be enough to remind you on a conscious level and give yourself assurance that healing was given to your sick friend. This will also be the case even if you were unable to recall any part of your astral journey.

23 Meditation To Release Fears From Previous Lives

Once in a while, illness occurs as a result of fears acquired from a previous life that have been encoded within the spirit body. These fears appear to be a very real part of the conscious mind and are quite naturally incorporated into the life now being lived. In these cases, an individual needs to face the fear by regressing to the past life. When this fear is conquered, valuable knowledge and skills will be released into the conscious mind for use in this life. It is, therefore, necessary to be aware of this factor and to do this meditation only when ready to face those fears that cannot be justified from this life alone.

- Lie in a comfortable position with your head well supported, your hands at your side and your feet outstretched. Breathe deeply and visualize yourself bathing in warm sunlight that represents God's love for you. Continue to breathe deeply, allowing your stress to be washed away by this light.
- Say your own prayer of protection and ask your spirit guides to draw close to you.
- Breathe slowly and deeply now and ask your spirit guides to lead you back into the life or lives that are affecting you now.
- Visualize all your Major and Minor Chakras one at a time and watch them open. Continue to breathe deeply and slowly. Watch any stress running down your body as thick black oil and see it leave through your foot chakras. Your body is now relaxed and your conscious mind is ready to begin your journey back in time.
- Take several deep breaths and attune to your spirit body. Let yourself feel this body as it glows and pulsates with life.
- Begin to search this body for any signs of stress. Many areas may feel tense. Observe this tension and allow yourself to focus on the part that feels acutely stressed.
- Concentrate on it and acknowledge how bad it feels. Breathe slowly and deeply. With previous lives in mind, allow your mind to become one with this area of your body. Watch this

part of your body as it manifests aches, pain, soreness, tingling or any other ill feeling. Continue to breathe deeply.

- Accept this discomfort and ask yourself what originally caused this feeling. Breathe deeply and wait for your mind to recall those pictures.

- Observe the answer as though watching a movie. Accept that this was done to you and watch your feeling (pain/ache/tingle) climax and then subside as you let go of your fears acquired in that life. (Example: A pain in the stomach gives rise to a picture of a sword stabbing you there. A fear of death arises. Accept this death as instant and painless.)

- Watch this feeling flow down your body as golden oil that passes away from you through your foot chakras. Breathe deeply and relax.

- Once again, begin to observe your spirit body and watch for new areas of tension. Continue to breathe deeply.

- Focus in on an area that seems most uncomfortable and once again allow your mind to recall pictures that will stimulate any further fears you need to release. Continue to breathe deeply and when the feeling climaxes once more, relax.

- You may continue to work on yourself until you have had enough.

- As the last climax occurs, attune to the sunlight and God's love. Visualize this light entering your body through the Crown Chakra. Breathe deeply and allow yourself to feel every part that you have worked on rejuvenating within itself.

- Now, allow yourself to create a new consciousness where fear has no place. Affirm to yourself that you are strong and courageous. Breathe slowly and deeply several times and sense this new awareness being stimulated within your spirit body.

- Know that this new discovery will be birthed into the conscious mind for you to use in your every day activities. Continue to breathe deeply as you attune to your physical body again.
- Visualize each Major and Minor Chakra closing and pull the muscles in over each one as you see it. Breathe normally and allow yourself to turn on to your side.
- Keep your eyes closed and allow your conscious mind to recall all the past-life pictures you have seen and the feelings that were released. When you are ready, sit up and write them down for further reference.

Note: Once you get the hang of this meditation, you may wish to survey your entire body. If so, simply begin by focusing on your big toe and when completed, move to each of the other toes on your right foot, one at a time. Then, pay attention to the soles, upper foot, ankle, calf, shin, knee, back of knee. Then focus in on your left big toe and repeat the procedure. Progress on up the body in this way until you reach the top of the head. Remember every part of your body will store a memory, so miss nothing. Many of these memories may relate to the same life. It will take you several months—maybe even years—to cover the entire body, so be patient.

24 MEDITATION TO CUT THE ETHERIC RIBBONS

When we begin life as a child, we are only attached by one etheric ribbon. That ribbon ties us to our mother. As the child grows, he becomes emotionally attached to his father, siblings, relatives, teachers, and others. This emotional attachment creates the ribbons that tie him to these people. These ribbons allow energy created from past interactions to flow backward and forward between the two. This stimulates them to repeat patterns of behavior that may seem routine or normal, although many of these behavior habits are painful and unnecessary. If you feel that this is the case with you, then you can free yourself with this meditation.

- Lie flat on your back with your hands laying by your side and take several breaths as you say your own prayer for peace.
- Take a long slow deep breath and feel your entire body relaxing. Take another, and imagine yourself standing in a floodlight that is God's light. Allow yourself to become a sponge and soak up this light. Feel your entire body relaxing even more as any stress or strain is washed away. Breathe deeply and slowly.
- Visualize yourself opening your Crown Chakras and relax the muscles that surround your skull. Breathe deeply and continue to open the other six chakras, remembering to take a deep breath between each.
- Now, open your Minor Chakras and breathe deeply. Call your spirit guides to your side and ask for their protection and guidance. Continue to breathe slowly and deeply.
- As you breathe in, visualize yourself becoming part of the white light that surrounds you. Know that you are lifting your vibration into a spiritual one.
- Create a picture of your mother standing before you. Breathe slowly and begin to scan her body. You are looking for a cord—it may take any form, such as a glass hose, a rope, ribbon, string, and so on. Follow this cord with your eyes; see it descending from your mother to the floor. If you have trouble visualizing, then trust your mind to know where it is

and approach it. Breathe slowly.

- Now, pick up the cord and begin to feel it. Look closely at it. Notice its size and weight. Begin to follow it towards yourself. This cord is very long and you may lose the image of your mother as you follow the cord. Do not be afraid. Breathe deeply as you leave your mother and begin to wind your way as though coming out of a dark cave.

- Continue to breathe slowly and look for a change in the cord's appearance. It may be a rope that suddenly becomes a ribbon. At this point of change, pause and notice your body's reaction. Notice how tense you have become. Breathe deeply and ask yourself why. Wait for your spirit guides to give you some images. As you see them, breathe deeply and try to interpret them. They may be very simple and direct or they may be symbolic. For example, a baby means dependency, a spider or crawly creature means childhood fears. Breathe deeply and slowly. Acknowledge that you no longer need this childhood memory and this fear or anxiety. Ask your spirit guides to take this fear away. Breathe slowly and feel yourself relaxing as you are healed.

- The cord is once again in your hands. Continue to follow the cord until it changes again. Breathe deeply and once again note your tension. Watch and understand the symbols that your spirit guides give you. Now, surrender to them for healing. Take several deep breaths and then continue to follow the cord. Know that you are coming close to yourself now. Breathe slowly and deeply as you begin to follow the cord up your body.

- Look for the point where the cord is joined to your body.

- Breathe deeply and gently take the cord in your left hand, which is the hand of unconditional love and look around for ascending stairs—if necessary, create them.

- Breathe slowly and climb these stairs. As you carry the cord, it may change weight. Acknowledge this change if it occurs and continue to climb. Breathe slowly and begin to look for your Higher Self at the top of the stairs. When you see your Higher Self, stand still, breathe deeply and see how wonderful your true self is, standing there to greet you. A perfect you, beautiful and complete. Invite this perfect you to assist you.

- Now, pay attention to the cord you are carrying. Create a knife in your mind and cut the cord as close to your body as possible. If you have trouble cutting it, acknowledge that you are afraid and ask your Higher Self to do it for you. Give yourself permission to let it be cut and wait. Breathe deeply and let yourself see hands coming towards the cord with something to sever it or pull it from you. Watch it happen. Hold your breath as it is severed and then breathe deeply as you are released. You are taking your first new breath of life.

- Now you are free. Climb the remaining stairs and embrace your Higher Self at the top of the stairs. Breathe deeply as you sense a completion with this union.

- Now, turn around and look down the stairs and say to yourself, "I am free. I am."

- Feel elated and let yourself breathe in life. Attune to your spirit guides and feel their joy in seeing you free. Thank them for helping you attain this joy. Breathe slowly and prepare to return to normal waking consciousness.

- Sense how much energy you have acquired. If it seems to be too much, send it as a ball of light to your mother to help her heal too. Bless your mother for having given you life.

- Begin to descend the stairs, visualizing yourself closing the Major and Minor Chakras. By the time you reach the bottom of the stairs, you will be aware of your physical body and the position in which you are lying.

- Breathe slowly and gently move yourself into a sleeping

position. Dream and know that you are making a new mindset and that you are now healing your Lower Self in mind, emotions, and physical body.

- When you wake up, write your findings down.

Note: This meditation can be done with father, lovers, husband, children and many more. Each person should be done individually. Don't hurry the process—it may take you several months, or even years, to work through all the relationships you feel it necessary to work through. But as each one is done, the results will manifest daily. The conditioned traps will fall away and freedom for self-involvement without guilt and judgment will arise.

MEDITATION FOR COLOR AND MUSICAL HEALING 25

Your entire being is made up of light and sound. This is the vibrational frequency that gives you solid form. When one is sick, this vibrational frequency is not in tune. By doing the following meditation you can correct your vibrational frequency by fine tuning it with music and color.

- Play your favorite meditation music as loudly as is comfortable.
- Lie on your back and say your own prayer for inner peace and oneness with God and your spirit guides.
- Relax and feel God's light flowing down and running through your entire body, pushing all stress out through your feet and into the ground. Take several slow deep breaths.
- Now, open the Major Chakras. Breathe deeply and know that

your spirit guides are with you. Listen and accept the music as part of the meditation. Feel the vibration of the music entering your body.

- Continue to breathe slowly and visualize God's white light descending and enveloping you.
- Receive this light into your body and watch it turn red. Know that this color is flowing into all your chakras. Feel it rejuvenating and stimulating your five bodies. Wait until a feeling of completion in achieved. Continue to breathe slowly and deeply.
- Now, watch as the color red turns to orange. Know that this color is flowing into all your chakras. Wait until a feeling of completion is achieved once more. Breathe slowly and deeply.
- Now, watch as the color orange turns to yellow and once more feel it flowing into all your chakras. Breathe deeply and wait once more for a feeling of completion.
- Listen to the music again and feel its vibration assisting these colors to flow throughout your body. Continue to breathe slowly.
- Now watch this color yellow become a beautiful healing green and once more feel it flowing into your chakras. Breathe deeply and allow yourself to feel this healing occurring. Lie there until a feeling of completion arises.
- Watch now, as green turns into blue and feel it flowing into your chakras. Listen to the music and feel its vibration having its effect on your vibration. Continue to breathe slowly and wait until a feeling of completion is achieved.
- Now, watch as blue turns into blue-mauve and know that it too is flowing into your chakras. Take a deep long slow breath and once more await a feeling of completion.
- Sense how the music flows through your body. Breathe

slowly and allow yourself to feel like flowing water. Watch as a pale lavender-pink color flows into your chakras. Feel it mingling with the flowing water that you have become. Know that your vibrational frequency is being healed. Wait until you feel a sense of completion. Be receptive now to a new frequency vibration that will stimulate you in the days to come.

- Watch as the higher colors of God are given to you. See the gold ray that envelops you. Wait for a feeling of completion.
- Now watch as God's color silver envelops you and wait for a feeling of completion. Know that your spirit body and Higher Mind Body are receiving healing. Breathe slowly and rejuvenate these bodies.
- Now watch as God's love embraces you as a peach color that will nurture your Higher Mind Body and Soul Body. Allow yourself to feel wise and loving as you embrace God.
- Allow God's form to touch you in the form of an electric blue ray that descends over and envelops you. Breathe slowly and feel his touch as the Holy Spirit. This is the final color that completes the healing.
- Allow yourself to flow into the music and drift with your thoughts as you lie and rejuvenate. Recognize yourself as sound and light and be one with God. Surrender yourself to God's will and be whole.
- As the music finishes, return your consciousness to your physical body by visualizing a rainbow and sliding down it until you reach your lower body.
- Once more, breathe deeply and again visualize God's white light flowing around and in you. Gently close all your Major and Minor Chakras.
- Thank your spirit guides and congratulate yourself on your healing work and move slowly, when ready, into a curled up position, ready to sit up.

Note: This meditation can also be applied to the physical body for repair of diseased organs. When meditating on the anatomy with color, always visualize the part to be healed before bringing in the relative color. Visualization helps the absorption to take place. The following is an outline of colors related to the physical anatomy.

- Red—Heart, blood, arteries and veins, liver, kidneys and rectum.
- Orange—Spleen, pancreas and small intestine.
- Yellow—Brain, eyes, gallbladder, lower bowel, stomach, duodenum, lymphatic system and bladder.
- Green—Nervous system, muscles, bone, tendons, enzymes and hormones.
- Blue—Lungs, throat, sinuses, ears and nose.
- Lavender—Genital organs, mouth glands, and reproductive glands.
- Purple—Entire body for solidifying new healing form.

26 Meditation To Deal With Obsession

Almost everyone, at some time during their life, has been obsessed by a goal, usually leading him or her into a situation involving a person or thing. While it is not wrong to be obsessed with a goal, it is wrong to be controlled by the obsessive ideas that restrict achievement of that goal. A negative obsession (believing in the obsessive ideas) can often ruin one's life because the negative aspects of any given situation seem to constantly get in the way and prevent achievement. To be a star in a movie could be a positive obsession, but if controlled by negative ideas, this dream could well be destroyed. The following meditation is designed to assist you to focus on the positive aspects of obsession and eliminate the bad ones.

- Relax into a comfortable chair with your back supported, feet on the ground, hands resting comfortably on your thighs, palms up.
- Become aware of your breathing and gently allow each breath to become slower and deeper until you have allowed all the tension of the day to leave you.
- Create a picture of yourself, alone, doing the thing that is your obsession. Allow yourself to become engrossed in this activity. (You should feel completely comfortable with yourself at this time.)
- Now bring other people into this picture. Allow your mind to create their characters. (They may be familiar people.) Notice your emotional reaction and your natural way of responding as they appear to invade your space. (Are you threatened, worried, anxious, tense, scared? These emotions will let you bring the negative ideas affecting you into focus.)
- Acknowledge what you feel. Accept this part of yourself as a process by which you have brought yourself to this point of realization. Allow yourself to know that you are no longer a child and that your life is filled with wisdom which can only lead you on towards your goal.
- Once again, recreate the scene of yourself, alone, doing the thing that is your obsession. Allow yourself to focus on the enjoyment you experience in reaching your goal. Recognize your creative power and your ability to express yourself. Recognize your body and your right to take up space in this

world. See yourself as the most important thing in your life—not the obsession of your goal. Breathe deeply as you awaken to the full realization of your power.

- Now visualize yourself expressing your obsession with emotional pleasure to those who had entered the previous visualization. See them listening to you and believing you. Listen to their responses and notice your new responses. Acknowledge that you have found a new way to communicate your obsession. (Your obsession will now appear to be less important).
- Breathe deeply, allowing your whole body to be filled with this new realization. Next, make a one sentence affirmation out loud, so that your conscious mind accepts this new identity that you have just awakened. Breathe deeply once again, and gently awaken to full consciousness.

Note: In time, this meditation may be used to overcome the need to have an obsession. Ideally, one who enjoys life lives in the moment and is not interested in obtaining any one particular goal.

27 MEDITATION TO GENERATE CONFIDENCE

At times, almost everyone could do with a boost to their ego, and gain a little more confidence in the way they express themselves. This meditation is designed to help you to do just that.

- Sit in a warm environment—in the sunshine or beside a fire.
- Breathe deeply, allowing the outside warmth to penetrate into the center of your being.

- Become aware of your Heart Chakra. Visualize a yellow rose (symbol of confidence) laying in the center of your chest. Watch it rise and fall as you breathe.
- As you begin to feel more relaxed and at ease with the rose, allow it to have animation. Watch it expand and grow as it becomes as large as your whole body. Allow it to envelop you within its petals.
- Feel the confidence it gives you. Now allow it to dissolve within your body and know that it is always with you.
- Say out loud: "I am confident."
- Take several long slow deep breaths, feeling the strength that this new-found confidence gives you.
- Allow yourself to come back to full consciousness.

Meditation For A Journey Into The Future 28

In the deep subconscious, all things are known—even what the future holds in store for you. Many of your future plans have already been laid out for you, waiting for you to tap into them. This meditation is designed to assist you to achieve a state of awareness that will allow you to unlock this inner wisdom and bring it into the conscious mind.

- Find a comfortable position, either lying on your back or sitting upright in a comfortable chair with your back and head well supported. Allow your hands to rest comfortably at your side.

- Take several deep inhalations, and expel the tension of the day.
- Focus on your Crown Chakra and visualize a halo totally surrounding your head and neck and expanding about 12 inches in circumference beyond your physical form.
- Visualize your Heart Chakra as an expanding ball of light extending 12 inches from your front and back as well as out to each side.
- Visualize your Base Chakra in the same way, allowing it to extend down to mid-thigh and up to the Solar Plexus Chakra.
- Become aware of your Spleen Chakra, running through from rear left to front right (a diagonal direction) and tell yourself to allow it to function productively.
- Decide what you would like to see about your future.
- Visualize yourself sitting or lying on a pink cloud that will take you forward in time. This cloud is your safe haven—you can return to it at any time and be nurtured and rejuvenated.
- Ask the cloud to take you forward in time. Allow yourself to feel it moving gently forward, like drifting in a boat.
- At this point, allow yourself to see colors as they manifest. The Third Eye Chakra will open naturally as you drift forward in time. Colors will come and go until you find yourself looking at a picture.
- Focus on this picture. Allow yourself to become one with it as you gently slide into its natural animation. The picture will become real. Allow yourself to be involved as you live your future activities.
- As you become more involved in your future, tell yourself often that you will remember what is occurring. To help yourself remember, carry a small notebook, and write single keywords in it.

- When you have finished exploring your future, place the book in a pocket over your heart, where you will store it for future recall.
- Climb back onto your pink cloud and allow it to caress and comfort you, especially if you have discovered something not necessarily to your liking. Feel the warmth of healing as the cloud gently begins to carry you back to the present.
- Allow yourself to feel its backward motion, and know that it will take you safely back to the security of your physical body.
- As you arrive back in the present, allow yourself to go over the information you have discovered about your future. If something makes you uncomfortable, recognize that this can be changed if you allow your conscious focus to change. Give yourself a moment to make a vow of change.
- Allow yourself to wake up. Turn or move into a comfortable position and allow yourself to dream about your discoveries. When you are ready, wake up and write everything down.

Note: Those seeking information about the future must be prepared for the unexpected. The conscious mind can be a liar and a cheat. The deep subconscious always reveals the truth. Maybe all the facts are not known, so be prepared to let some things go. Be ready to awaken to new things that will improve your situation.

29 Meditation To Work With Crystal Awareness

This meditation can be done with any kind of gemstone or natural crystal. Each stone will, according to its vibration, aid you in healing and balancing your five bodies, stimulating you to release negativity. Be prepared to discover new things about yourself, once you have done this meditation.

- Select relaxing meditational music and play it as loudly as you find comfortable.
- Lie on your bed or floor with your head comfortably supported.
- With both hands, hold the crystal you have chosen to work with on your Solar Plexus Chakra (located in your abdomen, just above the navel). If possible, the crystal should touch your skin, which allows an uninterrupted flow of energy from your hands to your body.
- Breathe deeply several times, as you relax into a calm state.
- Visualize God as a pulsating ball of white light above your head. Watch it suspended above your head for several minutes until you feel ready to join with it. Say aloud, "I am ready."
- As you give yourself permission to receive, watch the ball of light descend over you. Feel it touch the top of your head, face, neck, chest, and so on. As the light floods your entire body, attune to your arms. Feel this glorious energy running through your hands into the crystal. Feel the crystal resonating with this energy as the white light passes through it and into your Solar Plexus.
- Allow yourself to feel the music resonating in the crystal also. Watch the music dance through your body as the crystal resonates its tones.
- You will eventually reach a state of total peace. At this point, surrender to the love of God. Look above you once again in your mind's eye and see a golden light, fringed with electric blue, drifting down towards you. Visualize yourself reaching up to touch it.

- As your fingers reach it, become aware of how it is affecting you. Emotions will begin to flood your being. Let them be expressed. Do not try to understand them. Let yourself be cleansed of all old fear, anger, pain and guilt.
- Eventually you will settle into a stillness that will allow you to sleep. Dream on!

WORKING WITH METAPHYSICAL TOOLS 30

Metaphysical tools, whether tarot cards, rune stones, candles, or anything else, are merely aids for focusing the conscious mind. These tools often give individuals a feeling of comfort and confidence, which helps them to overcome any fears blocking enlightenment. Many wish to meditate but cannot relax enough to do so. If this is true for you, by using your favorite tool and this meditation, you will find it easier to grow in enlightenment.

- Dim the lights in the room. Take your favorite tool and place it on a table in a position where you can see the tool clearly.
- Seat yourself in a comfortable position directly opposite it, about three feet away.
- Say a prayer of protection, inviting the love of God and your spirit guides to draw close and assist you.
- Place both hands on your Solar Plexus Chakra. Feel the warmth of your hands flowing inward and upwards to your Heart Chakra. Breathe deeply.
- Now focus your eyes on your favorite tool. Let your eyes

explore it as though it is the first time you have ever seen it. Notice its shape, color, and size.

- Become aware of your hands. Feel the energy you are putting out as you explore your tool. Continue to look at the tool. As you gaze, your tool will begin to take on new shapes and meanings. Pictures will form in your head. Let it happen.
- When the feeling comes, allow your eyes to close. See your tool in your mind's eye. Watch it change its shape, size and form. Go with the flow—let yourself see what the tool wishes to reveal to you.
- When your tool has shown you its power and its uses, you will quite naturally want to open your eyes again. Do so. Look at your tool and acknowledge it for being your door opener.
- Say a prayer of thanksgiving to God and your spirit guides.

31 Meditation For Journeying Into Silence

Sometimes, no matter how much we try to still our minds, there are extraneous thoughts from the conscious mind that interrupt our focus of being still. This meditation is designed to assist you to enter that stillness and find the still, small voice of silence wherein lies wisdom.

- Sit comfortably in a cozy chair with your head supported, or lie propped up with pillows on the bed.
- Breathe deeply, letting the stress of the day leave you.
- Create a picture of a warm, sunny day in your head. Listen to

the birds singing in the trees, and allow yourself to know what they are saying.

- Create a picture of a snowy winter's day. Watch the snow falling and try to hear each snowflake as it lands. Listen to what they are saying.
- Create a picture of a fire crackling in the dark. Listen to the sounds of the fire and hear what it is saying.
- Create a picture of a babbling brook. Listen to the sound of the water as it gurgles by and hear what it says.
- Create a picture of the moon and stars. Listen to the silence of the heavens and the message they give you.
- Allow yourself to see darkness. Listen to its sound and the message it gives you.
- Allow yourself to see the light. Listen to its sound and the message it gives you.
- Spend time remembering all that you have heard and bring yourself back to the sounds of the room where you are in meditation. Listen to what it is telling you.
- Listen to what you are telling yourself, then gently rouse yourself to full consciousness.

32 MEDITATION FOR DEVELOPING PSYCHOMETRY

Psychometry is the ability to feel through the use of the spirit sense of touch. We touched our mothers this way and continue to touch every single person we meet in a similar manner. This meditation assists you to draw this skill into conscious awareness where you can more fully appreciate your feelings and those of others. This awareness results in better communication, increased productivity, and a better quality of life. When first working with this meditation, do not give in to fear. Fear can only cause you self-inflicted pain. Take the attitude you had as a child—that of playing in order to discover something new.

- Find a true friend and agree to work with them.
- Sit opposite one another on two hard chairs or upright on the floor. Place the chairs so that your knees are about 24 inches apart.
- Say a prayer of protection and call upon God's love to fill you both with joy.
- Each should then focus inward and open their Seven Major Chakras.
- By natural choice, one should sit quietly with eyes open. The other, with eyes closed, should then begin to explore the auric energy of the other by gently feeling around with fingertips and palms for electrical impulses. Do not touch the partner. When impulses are felt, the other should then take a turn.
- With eyes closed, each should now feel with their entire body the energy of the person sitting opposite. When body tingles are felt, this should be noted in silence.
- Allow these tingles to build. Notice their exact location and sense whether this is a good or bad feeling. Translate it into pain, stress, anger, joy, happiness, sadness, pleasure. Explore how each feels physically. Where are the aches and pains? There are many differences that can be explored.
- Continue to explore each other until you have had enough. Make a mental note of all you have discovered. The desire to

stop will be a mutual one which need not be expressed.

- With love, mentally thank your friend and visualize your own energy pulling back toward yourself. Watch this energy (various colors) moving back into your body until it has almost disappeared inside you.
- Both should then visualize the seven Major Chakras closing.
- Return to full consciousness. Sit further apart, and share your experiences. You will delight in finding out how sensitive and accurate each of you can be.

33 MEDITATION FOR DEVELOPING CLAIRAUDIENCE

Clairaudience is the spirit body's sense of hearing. As each of us is a spirit dwelling within a flesh-and-blood body, we all are capable of tapping into the spirit's five senses and using these senses on a conscious level to assist us in our daily lives. This meditation is designed to help individuals listen for spirit communication coming from loved ones who have passed on, spirit guides, or Master Teachers.

- Find a room where you will not be disturbed under any circumstance.
- Darken the room, or have a small lamp on to create a nurturing atmosphere.
- Lie or sit in a position that is open and comfortable.
- Begin to breathe deeply and slowly, allowing a natural rhythmic pattern to evolve.

- Visualize the Crown Chakra as a large ball of light. Sense it expanding 12 inches beyond its normal conscious resting place.
- Visualize the Third Eye Chakra as a smaller ball of light expanding outward and down, blending with the Crown and Throat Chakras.
- Visualize the Throat Chakra as a ball of light expanding to blend with the Heart Chakra. Now visualize the Heart Chakra as an even larger ball of light that swells to cover the others. As it does, it forms a large pyramid over you.
- Watch this pyramid grow and expand proportionately until it covers all of you. Then watch it expand upward toward God.
- Now mentally call out to your spirit guides or loved ones and ask them to speak to you. Sit and wait calmly, with an empty mind.
- After your conversation, watch the pyramid shrink. Close the Chakras and return to consciousness.

Note: They will communicate in one of three ways: 1) inside your head, sounding like your own voice or a comfortable, familiar voice; 2) inside your head as thoughts and dreams; 3) or you will hear them externally in very simple words. This will depend on what is most suitable for you to experience.

34 Meditation For Developing Clairsentience

Clairsentience is your spiritual sense of smell and taste. This skill is often neglected. When developed, it can be helpful in assisting you to know what foods are not good for your system. It also helps in awakening lost memories associated with food and drink. As children, we store these memories in the cellular neuromuscular memory. The awakening of these memories, which have been subtly controlling you as an adult, will help you to uncover many fears, pains, angers and guilts that may have resulted in allergies. The following meditation will help you to shed those childhood mindsets that were made without true awareness, and will leave you free to enjoy life.

- Sit comfortably in a chair which supports your back and allow yourself a few moments to relax by taking several deep breaths.
- Visualize yourself sitting at a table with food on it. Sit and contemplate being a child again. Imagine yourself shrinking in size until the food on the table is at eye level.
- Take special notice of all the food that your mind has placed on the table. (Your subconscious will choose those foods you need to know about.)
- With your mind, try to smell each of the foods. Take your time. Eventually, you will find yourself smelling them.
- When one of the foods seems to smell the strongest, see yourself eating that food. (You may well find yourself tasting that food as real.) As you eat the food in your mind, tell yourself that you will allow associations with the food to arise.
- Savor the smell and taste. Memories of when you last ate this food will arise. Allow yourself to recall the situation you were in at that time. Allow yourself to feel the emotions you had at that time.
- Acknowledge the situation and feelings, and look for any fear,

pain, anger, or guilt motivating you at that time.

- Now give yourself permission to let your mind drift back in time to earlier events when you were eating this very same food. (Several memories may arise. Look at each memory and find the common link.) As this occurs, the taste and smell of this food will grow stronger.
- Give yourself permission to dig further. Quell any fears that may arise in going back to your early childhood.
- Recreate the memory of being at the table looking at the food from eye level and tell yourself to remember the first time you ate this food.
- Allow the memory of the complete situation to arise. (You may well recall, in detail, things said and done that in some way scared you or made you angry.) Allow yourself to observe these events with the adult part of yourself. Do not try to be a child.
- Acknowledge your discovery and recognize that this situation was perceived by your child-self without true understanding.
- Allow the adult part of yourself to instruct the child-self by gently talking to yourself as you clarify the situation and heal the memory.
- Make a new premise concerning this food. Inform yourself that this food can be eaten without recurrence of your childhood experience.
- Allow yourself to smell and eat this particular food again and savor it as you do so.
- Allow yourself to feel the pleasure of eating this food and the confidence it brings to you.
- When you are ready, allow yourself to return to full consciousness.

- At a later date, try eating this food and watch your body's reaction. You should find that any allergies or emotional depressions will have disappeared.

Note: This meditation should not be done more than once a week. You need time to mentally and emotionally digest your findings and to adapt to the new concepts that you have made.

35 Meditation To Journey Into The Astral

During sleep, our spirits travel on the astral planes, though not everyone remembers their travels after awakening. The reason is that the conscious mind is fearful of dealing with unknown territories and will reject any "abnormal activities" even though it knows full well that astral travel has occurred. This meditation is designed to teach the conscious mind to accept and enjoy astral travel. (It will be necessary to lead yourself through most of this meditation without the assistance of a recorded tape.)

- Pick a time when you know you will not be disturbed and position yourself comfortably on your back on a bed or the floor. Support your head with a small pillow and allow your legs and arms to spread out diagonally a little from your body.
- Breathe deeply and relax your body. Allow all thoughts of your daily life to cease as you focus on your breathing.
- Become aware of your chakras and allow them to fully dilate by imagining each one to be a small hole that expands approximately ten times its original size. (Your subconscious

mind will automatically show you when each chakra is fully dilated.)

- In your mind's eye, look for a pathway that is to your liking (it can be any environment.) Begin to imagine yourself on this pathway. Look around and see what is there.
- Begin to walk down the pathway. Look at everything you see. Allow the things you focus on to be recorded into your conscious mind. Each object, plant or person is a symbol that can be analyzed later. (This part of the meditation allows the conscious mind to grow confident and feel involved.)
- Continue on the pathway. It will begin to ascend. Let yourself be excited and enthusiastic as you begin your ascent. Remind yourself that you know this pathway well and let yourself see the memory of what is ahead. Then give yourself permission to go on and find these places.
- At this point, allow yourself to know that your deep subconscious self will gently lead your conscious self forward and there is nothing to be afraid of. Continue on your journey, allowing yourself to feel and see more and more as you go forward. Eventually, everything you see and feel will become three-dimensional and real. You will then be out of body and truly on the real pathway.
- Your spirit self will know exactly where you want to go and what you want to do. In the blink of an eye, you will be there. Your conscious mind will observe with interest everything you do. During your journey, keep informing the conscious mind how wonderful it is to do what you are doing and the importance of remembering your experience.
- When it is time to return, allow yourself to find your pathway. The journey back will be far, far quicker than your original journey upward. Stand at the beginning of the pathway and go over everything that you have done. Once again, remind the conscious mind how wonderful and important this jour-

ney has been and then begin to return down the pathway.

- You will experience a pulling sensation drawing you into your body, where you will fall into a dream state. At the exact moment that you return to your body, inform the conscious mind that it will remember everything you have experienced and allow yourself to dream the memory.

- When you have done this meditation several times, you will begin to awaken immediately upon return to your body. Your body may seem immobile. Allow time for your body to wake up; when you can move, write your memories down. This allows the conscious mind to accept your experience as real.

- Recall the faces and objects you saw on the beginning of your journey. Allow your conscious mind to understand their symbolic meanings. In the days to come, they will make sense.

MEDITATION FOR REBIRTHING YOURSELF 36

No one is more capable of rebirthing you than yourself. After all, your spiritual self knows your lower self better than anyone else and is, therefore, most capable of helping you through a transition. As in a real birth, you need assistance, and your Master Teachers will be there to help you. This meditation should only be done at times when you feel you are ending a cycle and beginning a new one.

- Choose a time when you will be on vacation or separated from friends and family. (This process takes time, just as a real birthing does.)

- Consciously prepare for your rebirthing by carrying out several rituals that are important to you—taking a bath, singing songs, eating favorite foods, and so on.
- Fill the room with lighted candles, warm lights and music. Make the room warm and cozy.
- Sit in the room and contemplate the importance of this rebirthing ceremony. Confirm that you are ready to move on to the next cycle of your life.
- Remove your clothing and lay down on a comfortable bed with a sheet or warm blanket over you.
- Begin to breathe slowly and deeply, allowing yourself to feel the warmth of the bed and the room.
- Open your Major Chakras. Attune to God and your spirit guides in prayer. Ask for assistance.
- Visualize yourself dressed in special robes and acknowledge this special occasion. Recognize your wisdom and power to make decisions. Decide what you would like to do in this next cycle and create tools to bring with you that will assist you—a crystal for clarity, a flute for truth, a rope for power, etc.
- Allow your mind to lead you as you imagine yourself inside the womb. Notice that the tools you have chosen are with you. Lose all sense of time. Allow yourself to lie in many positions until you find yourself in the fetal position.
- Hold the tools in your hands and allow yourself to prepare for birth. Await the natural urge to stretch out. The early urges will be weak. Stretch a little and relax. Feel all the sensations that arise, and affirm to yourself that you are doing well. Feel the presence of your spirit guide waiting to assist you.
- Recognize the birth canal by visualizing a white light that seems to attract you. In your mind, move towards it. The desire to physically move will continue to arise. Resist any

desire at this point to cease the rebirthing process. Natural fears will arise and you should remind yourself that there is nothing to be afraid of as you hold the tools you have chosen.

- Let the moment continue as the light draws you upward. When the urge to stretch becomes paramount, allow yourself to stretch up and out. Say mentally, then aloud, "I am free."
- Focus on the tools that you have brought and remind yourself of the choices they represent. Allow yourself to feel confident.
- Attune to the joy you feel and your spirit guides who have delivered you into this new cycle of life. Recognize that this new birthing has brought you into a state of wisdom which cannot be denied.
- Allow yourself to fall asleep for awhile. (Your conscious mind will adapt to the new you in dream form.)
- Awaken and wrap a new towel around you and then drink something pleasant-tasting. Confirm to yourself that you are newborn and have a new start in life. (These physical actions help the conscious mind accept what has happened to you.)

Note: This meditation is a spiritual one, but its importance lies in the physical effect it causes and should not be confused with erasing history. Full memory will remain and life will be the same. It is your perception of life that will change.

MEDITATION TO ERASE SHOCK AND FEAR 37

There comes a time in everyone's life when the awareness of shock and pain becomes conscious. Usually, individuals feel completely depressed and unable to assist themselves to induce a happy and fulfilled life at this time. By erasing the shock and fear that has been stored in the cellular neuromuscular memory, a normal, carefree happy life can be obtained. Unlike the earlier meditation given in this book, where intense study is done over several meditations with conscious awareness, this one can be done without knowing the original cause of the shock or fear. This meditation should be done when you are ready to surrender to yourself and the healing power of God.

- Say a prayer of protection and ask God for help.
- Reach out in your mind for your spiritual Master Teacher guides to assist you.
- Visualize yourself in a deep dark forest, where you cannot see clearly. Accept the darkness that surrounds you and wait.
- Listen to the noises of the forest. Let yourself jump with each sound and let yourself be afraid.
- Cry out in your mind for someone to come to your assistance and wait patiently. (Your fear will build—go with the flow.)
- Let your mind show you monsters in the darkness in the same way it did as a child.
- Look for a patch of light within the darkness. Watch that light grow in intensity as it comes towards you and allow yourself to be curious about it.
- Look within the light and find someone there. When you feel at ease with this person, enter into the light and stand beside them.
- Begin to have a conversation with this person. Ask who they are and what they are going to do for you. Ask them to lead you out of the forest.

- As you speak with them, acknowledge that this is your spiritual Master Teacher guide, who has come to your rescue. Listen to their advice. Be the little child, with wide eyes and open ears, and absorb the confidence and love this spirit guide gives you.
- When you are ready, your spirit guide will take your hand and lead you through the dark forest. Your spirit guide will point out things to you and help you see that many of the things you thought were evil or bad are in fact something quite different. (Many of the visions you perceive will be symbolic. Ask for interpretations if you do not understand).
- As you move through the forest, you will notice it is becoming brighter. By the time you leave the forest you will be in broad daylight. Stand and look back at the forest and see it as it really is. You will be surprised at what you see.
- Acknowledge how out of proportion your view of life has been and vow to see things clearly in the future.
- Embrace your spirit guide and receive God's love in an act of healing. Then thank them and return to full consciousness.

Note: Choose the relative gender of your spirit guide when preparing your tape.

MEDITATION TO TAP INTO SOUL FEARS 38

Everyone is born with soul fears. These fears are necessary as they stimulate each individual to aspire towards becoming one with the Creator. By working consciously with the five soul fears, one can achieve a great deal in life.

These fears are: The fear of Ascension—Success. The fear of Descending—Failure. The fear of Separation—Isolation. The fear of Assimilation (Being the Center)—Responsibility. The fear of Divine Unconditional Love—Acceptance of All Things. This meditation will help you to find out which fears you are using in this life.

- Relax in a comfortable position with your head and back supported.
- Let your mind focus on someone or something that is important to you at this time.
- Have an imaginary conversation with this person or thing where you explain yourself and your needs.
- Allow them to refuse your requests and notice your emotional response. (Allow a long pause before proceeding with this section of the meditation.) If you are angry and feel you have been cast out, you have touched the soul fear of separation. If you are miserable and feel you have failed to communicate your needs, you have touched the soul fear of descending. If you are in emotional/physical pain you have touched the soul fear of divine unconditional love. If you feel rejected and want to ask again, you have touched the soul fear of ascension. If you can feel and understand the position of your imaginary person/thing and while accepting it feel something else too, then you are touching the soul fear of assimilation.
- Accept yourself and what you have uncovered. Recognize that this new information will assist you to see things with clarity in the future and allow you to make choices you would not have made before.
- Dissolve the visual picture you have created. In its place, create the picture of a room. In this room lies a book of wisdom. Go to the book and read a page. Look for words or

a picture. Acknowledge that this information is true. Allow yourself to perceive clear directions on how to focus yourself when dealing with future issues stemming from the use of this soul fear.

- Breathe deeply, and allow your conscious mind to assimilate this new information.
- Now, focus on your breath and allow your body to relax as it releases old conscious fears that have been stored in the cellular neuromuscular memory. Observe the memories that arise as you let go. Continue to breathe slowly and deeply.
- Watch your body spasmodically twitch as it releases old stresses. Breathe deeply. Relax.
- Allow your body and mind to drift into sleep and when you are ready, awaken feeling refreshed and revitalized.

MEDITATION FOR FACING EMOTIONS 39

There are three kinds of people on this planet—those who live in their minds; those who live in their emotions and those who live in both. Your everyday conditioning, based on frequently misunderstood role models you have experienced in this life, cause you to create barriers for self-protection and self-preservation. This meditation will assist you to remove those barriers and awaken to your true feelings. Use twice weekly on an indefinite time schedule.

- Place yourself in beautiful surroundings—a cozy room, or out in the park. Lie on your back and contemplate letting go of your life as you know it.

- Breathe deeply, inhaling the beauty that you feel surrounds you and exhaling the stress and tension from your body.
- Open all seven chakras by visualizing white light flowing into each of them. (The sun can be used to help visualize). Breathe deeply until you feel totally relaxed and unable to move.
- Acknowledge that your physical body is asleep. (You may hear yourself breathing or snoring.)
- Allow your mind to flow and watch pictures of incidents from your life run across your Third Eye Chakra. These incidents will have a common factor—an emotion. Acknowledge this emotion and move into your feeling.
- Let this emotion run through your entire body and watch your body react in many ways, as you release this false emotion created by your mind to justify your means.
- Allow yourself to breathe deeply again. Let the body relax as you move into the second stage of this meditation.
- Become aware of your body and its position. Tell yourself that you are now looking at and feeling your spirit body that lies within the physical body. (It will feel just as solid.)
- Allow your mind to home in on your Heart Chakra. Let yourself visualize it as a tiny white rosebud.
- Watch the bud begin to grow and open up until it is in full bloom. Acknowledge that your Heart Chakra is now fully dilated. Feel the true emotions that will arise.
- Think of the same things that had arisen from your mind earlier and the emotion you had felt. Allow your spiritual self to give you the real emotion. Do not try to guess—wait and let it arise.
- Now visualize someone coming toward you. Reach out to this

person and tell them how you feel. Allow yourself to be comforted by them until this emotional feeling is replaced with happiness and strength.

- Feel the bond you have created with this person and know they are with you always. Allow yourself to know the changes you have made in yourself by feeling them.
- Breathe deeply, letting yourself accept the new you. Let yourself gently become aware of your Heart Chakra. Allow the rose that you saw earlier to go inside the chakra, disappearing inside the body. Close the chakra and seal it with love.
- Close all other chakras, except the Crown Chakra. Allow this to remain slightly open. To do this, visualize a halo around your head. Know that you are now permanently in touch with your higher self and God.
- Gently bring yourself back to full waking consciousness and take fluids into your body. Later, take a bath and contemplate the new you. (Water recharges your battery, so to speak.)

40 Meditation To Face The Real Self

At times, we may find ourselves wondering who we really are. This meditation is designed to assist you to unveil the real you who wishes to be expressed without hindrance of earthly ways.

- Sit in a comfortable arm chair, hands laying gently on your lap and legs uncrossed. Take several slow, deep breaths.
- Allow yourself to open the Third Eye Chakra by releasing the

tension in the face and brow. Breathe deeply and give yourself permission to open this chakra.

- Visualize a person coming towards you. It may be male or female. (This is your Higher Self.) Ask this person to show you something of interest and acknowledge their leadership.
- Follow them to a place of interest, where you will observe and ask questions of them. Allow yourself to learn from them.
- When you have completed this conversation, embrace this person and feel yourself melting into them as you accept the unity of your Higher and Lower selves becoming one. Look about you and recall all you have learned.
- Look for a flight of stairs and climb them until you come to the top. Here you will find your spirit guides waiting for you. Walk with them and ask more questions and learn.
- Now, embrace them and allow yourself to melt into them in the same way as with your Higher Self. Let yourself become one with them as you bond in love. (This will change your vibration and level of consciousness.)
- Return to the stairs. As you descend, you will return to a state of awakened consciousness. When you do so, write down your discoveries.

41 Meditation For Unconditional Love

Everyone has a built-in urge to seek unconditional love from their partners and friends, as well as from God. Few ever really obtain a full realization of this wonderful feeling of unconditional love. This meditation is designed to assist you to feel God's love within the body and to take it into your daily life practices, which will result in better relationships.

- Have meditation music playing softly. Sit in a comfortable position. Relax and breathe in time with the music.
- Visualize yourself in the middle of a large field of corn. As you look in every direction, you see nothing but corn for miles and miles. Acknowledge that you are completely alone. Feel the warmth of the sun penetrating your body as you relax into a sleepy state.
- Allow your mind to recognize the symbolic form that God takes as the sun that warms you. Become aware of a gentle breeze that caresses your body as you lay there in the sun. Listen to the sound of the breeze in the corn. Recognize that the breeze is the hand of God that touches you. Lie and receive his touch.
- As you lay there on this warm sunny day, notice that the sun is beginning to cast a bright shaft of light on you. As you bathe in this light, open your Heart Chakra and allow yourself to feel all the love that God gives you. Recognize that He loves you for all that you are. Know that there is no judgment, only acceptance.
- Allow yourself to see in the light. Look for someone who is standing next to you. (This will be your interpretation of God.) Take their hand and hear them tell you how much they love you. Feel your response. Let yourself cry with joy. Know that you have come home. Embrace them and feel their healing hand flowing through your body.
- As the shaft of light fades, lie there and once again enjoy the warmth of the sun. Allow yourself to keep sensing the feelings of unconditional love. (Your mind will accept this feeling.)

- Acknowledge that God will always speak to you through the sun, wind and natural surroundings of this earth. Make a promise to yourself to seek these places of comfort and allow yourself to feel God's gentle hand every time the wind touches you.

- Know that when you hold another in your arms, you will be holding God, and that they in return will be God holding you. Acknowledge the reverse of this and know that you will give to others in the same way.

- Allow yourself to contemplate this understanding. Close your Heart Chakra and return to normal waking consciousness.

42 MEDITATION ON THE TRINITY

This meditation is a very powerful one. It allows you to become conscious of the three aspects of God—the Father, the Son and the Holy Spirit. When you are attuned to all three aspects, the creative self can manifest whatever is asked for. This meditation helps you become whole and acquire physical things in life that will assist you on your pathway. It should not be used to manipulate or control others. This meditation must be done in unconditional love, surrendered to the will of God, which will be your will also.

- This would be a good time to use a copper pyramid if you have one. If not, place yourself in the center of a warm room, and imagine that the perimeter of the room is the base of the pyramid.

- **Close your eyes and breathe slowly and deeply, allowing the stress and tension of the day to leave you. From each corner of the room, create the copper pyramid. See the poles coming out and upward in a diagonal slope to meet over the top of your head.**

- Allow yourself to visualize the edges of the copper pyramid becoming an electric blue radiant light. Feel protected and at peace within this environment.

- Now visualize the pyramid as a two-dimensional, equilateral triangle. Notice its radiant electric blue light shining in the darkness. With your mind's eye, add gold along the outer edges so that a second triangle is formed. (The blue represents the Holy Spirit; the gold represents God.)

- In your mind's eye, place yourself in the left-hand corner of the triangle. Place the person or object of your desire in the right hand corner. Watch the Holy Spirit manifest in the top apex as a cloud.

- Repeat these words out aloud: "I am one with God and God is one with me. I am one with the person/object and the person/object is one with me. The person/object is one with God and God is one with the person/object. The person/object is one with me and I am one with them. God is one with me and God is one with the person/object."

- Having perceived all aspects of giving and sharing, now visualize yourself, God, as the Holy Spirit cloud and person/object coming together in the center of the pyramid. Hold the person/object and feel the cloud surrounding you both. Acknowledge the oneness that you feel.

- Let yourself know that this act of surrender and unity will bring a positive change into your life which will help others, and bring your hopes and dreams into reality.

- Say out loud, "So be it." Feel the emotions you have unleashed in knowing that you have created something with God/person/object's help. Prepare to receive it in the flesh.

- Gently bring yourself back to the room. Notice how reverent you feel. Savor this awareness and know that it will take time for what you have asked for to come into your hands.
- Acknowledge your patience and know that it will happen when you are fully prepared to receive what you have asked for. Promise to use what is given to you as well.
- Spend quiet time for about one hour planning those moves that will bring what you have asked for into your life.

43 Meditation For Past-Life Regression

There are times when we all wonder whether we have lived before. Our imagination may run away with us as we find ourselves remembering various incidents in history as though we were there. Our emotions often give us a clear sense of bonding with that time and the mind immediately tries to find the cause by looking into the information we have received in this life about the past.

Why do we do this? The answer is simply to stimulate ourselves to unlock inner wisdom. Any wisdom that arises, may at first seem insignificant, but as time goes on, a great deal more is released from the deep subconscious into the conscious mind.

Often, the deep subconscious mind will release the negative aspects of a life first. These will then stimulate the conscious mind to search for deeper answers. These negative

aspects will still be present in your life now and must be cleared in order to release the positive traits of a previous lifetime.

Note: To do this meditation, it is important to have a recorder handy, so that you can listen to it later.

- Sit comfortably in a chair, so you will not fall asleep.
- Begin your deep breathing exercises and allow yourself to relax.
- Say a prayer of protection and open your major chakras. Attune to your spirit guides, who will assist you on your journey.
- Allow yourself to feel their presence and the confidence that you can do this meditation. If you cannot find this feeling, do not continue. You are too afraid. If ready to proceed, say out loud, "I am ready, and will speak out loud as much as I can." Make a mental note to use keywords that will stimulate your conscious memory after this meditation.
- Allow yourself to leave your house and come across a small rowing boat on a river. (The river is the sea of life and the boat is your safe haven.) Get into the boat and sit in a comfortable position, so you can see where you are going.
- Look behind you and see that your spirit guides are steering the boat, taking you to the life that is most suitable for you to view at this time. Sit back and enjoy the ride.
- As you drift down the river, various scenes will unfold for you to look at. They will be events from this life. Watch with interest, but do not get emotionally involved—if you do, your journey will end there.

- You will enter a dark part of the journey as you pass from this life to the next. Notice if you are afraid, and the feelings you have. Push them aside and joyfully move on.

- You will come into the light and a new set of scenes. Watch them as before. If you are emotionally drawn to become involved with one of them, you will be there. (It is your emotions that bond you with the past life, not your mind.)

- When you find yourself being pulled to the river's edge, climb out of the boat and look around. See that your spirit guides are still with you. Allow yourself to relive this life. Let your conscious mind observe as you explore. Notice the emotions you feel. Recognize that these emotions are still present in your existing life. Look at your clothing. Watch how you act and conduct yourself with others. Look for talents, skills, strengths that you had then. Find the fears that you conquered too. Allow yourself to know what year it is and where you are. Savor every moment spent in this life.

- When you have seen and learned all that is relative to your existing life, you will be naturally drawn back to the boat. Climb aboard, and notice your spirit guide's presence. Ask if there is more to see. If there is, the journey will continue. Each time you leave and return to the boat, check that your spirit guides are with you. (This ensures that you will not drift off into fantasy and dreams.)

- When you have obtained all the information you need, your spirit guides will turn the boat around and slowly bring you back to your present life. Visualize yourself now lying down in the boat, and allow yourself to recall all that you have discovered about yourself. If you have any questions about what you have seen, ask your spirit guides and listen to their simple answers.

- As you journey back to this time, you will enter a brightly lit area on the river. This is the beginning of your present life.

Allow yourself to notice and feel the importance and spiritual power you have within you as you journey through this light.

- The boat will come to the river bank. Step out and thank your spirit guides for journeying with you. Promise to meet again soon and allow yourself to walk away from the river towards your house. As you approach your house, recall all that you have seen in the meditation once more.
- Open your front door and be in your room. Awaken feeling refreshed.
- Record all that you remember onto the tape recorder. At a later time, go back and listen to the entire tape. Expect new memories to arise on a conscious level. These should be written down for future reference.

MEDITATION TO FIND A SAFE PLACE 44

This meditation is designed to allow you to escape the pain and suffering of the world, whether caused by people or your status in life, and to gather strength to return to your life with renewed hope, passion and drive to improve your situation.

- Sit in a chair, legs uncrossed, arms resting gently on your lap. Take several deep breaths, exhaling tension and stress.
- Ask your spirit guides to draw close to you and say a prayer quietly to yourself asking for God's love and protection.
- Allow yourself to find a pathway and begin to walk along it. Eventually you will arrive at a beautiful place where water

flows, flowers bloom, and birds sing. Look for a place to sit and soak up the atmosphere. Wait patiently for someone to come to you.

- Your spirit guides will appear in a form that is familiar to you. Invite them to sit with you.

- Allow them to talk to you through an inner meditation of their choosing. This meditation will strengthen and rejuvenate you. Know that you can come here any time you choose, and that your spirit guides will always come to assist you.

- Spend time talking with your spirit guides about your problems. Listen to their advice.

- Allow yourself to know that you will remember this advice when you are fully conscious. When your time with them is completed, return along your pathway. Allow yourself to return to full consciousness.

45 Meditation To Touch The Fairy World

Children believe in fairies, elfins, goblins and gnomes, but few ever get to see them. Hence, the adult world thinks them non-existent. This meditation is designed to assist you to prove to yourself that they do indeed exist. Before attempting this meditation, it is important to be in a peaceful, serene state. You do not wish to project your negativity and attract gremlins and ghouls. So do this meditation on a warm sunny day when you have nothing better to do than attune to God's paradise, this world called Earth.

- Take a trip into the country. Select a quiet day when there will not be hoards of visitors there too.
- Find a nice spot, where the grass is green, and the foliage is abundant.
- Sit awhile and attune to the energy surrounding you. With your mind, gently call out to the creatures of the earth to surround you with peace and love. (These creatures are the friends of the fairy kingdom and must not be taken lightly.)
- Prop yourself up against a tree, or a low seat and quietly watch the area around you for signs of life.
- When your inner feelings tell you to close your eyes, do so. Breathe deeply, allowing your spirit body and senses to overcome the physical ones. (Remember that the crossover cannot be felt, but the spirit body consciousness will feel lighter and brighter than normal).
- Let your spirit body sense your environment and search for a direction to focus on. Your spirit body can sense the presence of fairies. When the feeling is extremely strong, gently allow your eyes to half open.
- Gazing through your eyelashes, you will perceive something. Watch closely. What may appear to be a fly might well be something else. A tree stump may hide a gnome, a blade of grass may hide a pixie.
- Allow your heart to reach out to whatever you see. Be receptive to feeling some response. Allow the fairy world to attune to your vibration. With your mind, gently invite them to approach you. Do not move.
- If it is their will, they will come and allow you to see them. They will not come if you're steeped in disbelief. You must have the heart and soul love for them that a small child would have.

- Some will fly, some will walk and some may even talk. Enjoy what they show you and allow yourself to learn about them.
- When they have had enough, they will simply leave. Allow yourself to move into a fully awakened conscious state, where you will appreciate the fairies' work in keeping this world in balance with the laws of nature.

46 Earth, Air, Fire And Water Meditation

Though we are surrounded by these natural elements, we rarely recognize their power over us and the lessons they teach us. This meditation is designed to bring you into that awareness and use them to cleanse yourself. This meditation affects all five bodies and should be done two or three times a year.

- Light four candles and place one in a position aligned with the four points of the compass.
- Place a bowl of earth somewhere inside the square that the four candles form. Place a second bowl full of water exactly opposite it, allowing room for yourself to sit between them in a crosslegged position facing north. Acknowledge the presence of air which you breathe as the fourth element.
- Breathe deeply and fill your lungs with this air. Look at the flame of the candle in front of you and acknowledge its power over you. Look at the earth and acknowledge its power over you. Sense the water and acknowledge its power over you too. Acknowledge that your body is made of these four elements.

- Close your eyes and begin the meditation. Breathe deeply, calling upon the air to clear away any mental cobwebs. Visualize these cobwebs across your face and watch them disappear.

- Breathe deeply again, and call upon the fire to engulf you in its flames and cleanse you of impurities. Visualize yourself entering a large blue flame and watch your body sparkle and glisten as the flame cleanses you.

- Breathe deeply again, and call upon the earth to balance your energies. Visualize yourself standing up to your neck in soil, which gently caresses you. Pour some over your head and face, and watch it gently fall away.

- Breathe deeply again and call upon the water to cleanse you of negative emotions. Visualize yourself bathing in it and swimming under water. Watch your negative emotions drift away as your body moves through the water.

- Visualize a small pile of earth, upon which a small fire burns. Sense the air feeding life into the flames. Watch the water evaporate into steam, and see them all working together. Know that these elements are doing the same for you and that all five bodies are in harmony.

- In reverence, thank these four elements for the healing they have given you.

- Acknowledge their power. Visualize fire in its mightiest forms, and recognize the voice of God within it. Visualize water as the ocean and rivers that separate the land and once more recognize God's powerful form. Each has a voice. Listen to the message that each gives you.

- Visualize the Earth, its mountains and valleys and the winds that blow through them. Recognize God's beauty expressed in them and listen to their voices and God's message for you.

- Recognize that this power and beauty that you see in the

elements is also within you. Accept this power and beauty as your heritage.

- Thank the elements for being one with you, and ask for their continued support. Open your eyes, and gently touch the flame, earth, water and air. Consciously thank God for this time of healing.

- Blow three candles out and place the remaining one in a safe place where it can burn down. Set the bowls of water and earth on either side of it in an act of reverence. Later you can douse the candle and return the water and earth to their proper places.

47 Meditation To Open The Inner Eye

Many achieve the opening of the Third Eye Chakra, but few manage to open the Inner Eye, which allows perception to be three-dimensional. In simple terms, the opening of the Inner Eye allows one to perceive things as though they are real and can be held in the hand, while the Third Eye Chakra merely gives an impression of something seen. Before one can open the Inner Eye, one must first overcome the many fears that have been acquired from early childhood. I suggest you practice many of the other meditations in this book before attempting this one.

- Sit comfortably in a darkened room and prepare yourself as in the basic meditations. Open all your major chakras and attune to God and your spirit guides.

- Now focus on your forehead. Feel the tension held there. Relax the muscles and allow yourself to visualize your forehead from deep within the brain.

- This deep place within the brain is your pineal gland, which is sensitive to light vibrations that come from your spiritual self and the spirit world. Spend a moment feeling it with your emotions. (If fear arises, try to cast it from you. If the fear is too strong, end the meditation.)

- Continue to acknowledge your strength as you begin to stimulate the pineal gland to function, by desiring to see outward from your brain. Visualize a small crack of light in the distance which you know is outside of yourself.

- Focus on the light and allow yourself to be drawn towards the light. As you move toward the light, know that your Third Eye Chakra is already open and receiving images from outside yourself. Recognize that you are cutting a pathway from the pineal gland to the frontal lobes of your brain where your sensory nerves are functioning.

- Give yourself permission to see clearly.

- As you draw closer to the light, imagine you are looking through a pair of binoculars. Turn the dial slowly and allow the binoculars to focus. This allows your physical eyes to be a part of the action. Rapid eye movement will result. When focused, they will relax.

- Now that your physical eyes are in focus, allow your Third Eye Chakra to relay the information of light patterns back to the pineal gland. Allow the pineal gland to tune in and reveal the true picture. This may well be a spirit guide or something belonging to them which will be easy for you to look at.

- Once you have achieved your goal of using your inner eye, it may well close immediately. If so, thank your spirit guide, close your chakras and end the meditation. You may acquire a headache—this is not unusual. Sleep and let your body heal.

- If your Inner Eye remains open, proceed with an open heart and mind to discover a new world where vision takes on a new dimension for you. Look at the auras of your spirit guides, the various hues and colors, the many things that they would show you. Continue looking until your spirit guide tells you to cease. Gently end the meditation by closing the Third Eye Chakra, and then the rest of your Major Chakras and return to normal waking consciousness.

- Write your experiences down for future reference. Much of what you will have seen will be symbolic in some way to help you in the future.

48 Meditation To Express The Full Self

To express the full self means to act in a physical way in which all five bodies are functioning at their optimum capability. To do this, you must first obtain a complete mental rapport with your emotional self. Next, acquire a complete trust of your spiritual self and the inner wisdom that flows from your Higher Mindbody. When these four bodies are in alignment, attunement to the God self, where all things are felt and loved unconditionally, will become your natural desire. The following meditation will assist you to acquire that goal.

- Fast for twelve hours, drinking only water and fruit juices.

- Pick a time when you will not be disturbed for several hours.

Lie in a comfortable position with your head well supported, legs stretched out about one foot apart, and hands at your side. Breathe deeply and generally relax the muscles throughout your body.

- Open the Major Chakras and the Minor Chakras of the hands and feet. Breathe slowly and deeply, allowing yourself to sink into the bed.
- Become aware of your physical form and watch it slowly fall asleep until you feel you cannot move. Breathe deeper.
- Attune to the energy in your Base Chakra and allow the sexual energy to build there. (This sexual energy will climax without physical help.) As you orgasm, feel this energy flowing into the etheric body.
- Breathe deeply and attune to the energy in your etheric body. Focus on the Solar Plexus and watch the energy build. You will sense prickles and tingles all over your body, building into an orgasm. Allow this energy to flow into your spirit body.
- Breathe deeply and attune to your spirit body. Focus on your Heart Chakra and watch the energy build as you begin to glow all over with warmth. Allow it to build into an explosive orgasm of pure joy.
- Breathe deeply and attune to your Higher Mind body. Focus on your Throat and Brow Chakra. Watch the energy build in your body as you sense yourself beginning to feel like flowing water. Allow it to orgasm into an explosion of light. (You will leave your body and find yourself standing somewhere in the room. You will be aware that you are spirit.)
- Allow yourself to look at your sleeping physical body. With your spirit mind, feel your physical body looking at yourself.
- Then, with your spirit body, look for your ascended self standing a little above you and off to the side. Allow your

spirit body to feel your ascended self looking at you.

- Recognize that all three aspects of yourself are looking at one another from each position and that all perspectives are perceived and felt from every angle as one experience. Know that you are bonding your lower self with your higher self. (This is a unique experience that can only be achieved once or twice in a lifetime.)

- Savor the bonding and allow your spirit self to return to the body, carrying with it the memory of this bonding experience.

- Allow your physical self to awaken. Write down your experiences for future reference and then go to sleep. (Sleeping allows the conscious mind to digest this experience and accept your changed vibration and perspective on life.)

49 Meditation To Journey To Other Worlds

Many people believe we are not the only creatures to inhabit a planet, but few believe in the existence of beings with abilities equal to or greater than our own. One way to find out is to astral travel to those places where it is physically impossible to go. Unfortunately, most of us are too scared on a conscious level to find out, so little research is done in this area. If you have the desire to find out for yourself, there is no limit to how far you can travel when out of body. Your spirit self knows the places to go. If you intend to do this meditation, recognize that you must already have a conscious mindset that believes in extraterrestrials.

- Prepare yourself several days in advance by imagining yourself leaving your body and going to a foreign planet. Your conscious mind must learn that there are no limits to its enquiries.

- As in other meditations for astral travel, prepare yourself on the day according to your personal discipline. When ready, sit in a comfortable chair with your head supported.

- As in the meditation for general astral travel, allow yourself to go through the steps until you find yourself outside of your body.

- Reaffirm to your spirit mind that you wish to connect with extraterrestrials that will benefit your spiritual growth. (There must be a purpose to your quest.)

- Your spiritual self will give you choices from familiar places you have visited before, but have not remembered consciously.

- Select the one that feels right. Allow your spiritual self to take you there by giving yourself permission to leave.

- Allow your conscious mind to notice how sure and secure your spiritual self is as you make your way through the heavens. Notice how fast you move and acknowledge the power of your spirit self as it overcomes time and space in the blink of an eye. (This is one time you will experience movement as you journey from point A to point B. Normally, travel is instantaneous.)

- Focus on the planet and notice how it looks from space. Watch yourself arrive. Ask yourself what you know about this planet. Let your spirit self lead you to a place that is comfortable. Wait to make contact with the inhabitants of this planet.

- Whoever they are, they will be friendly and supportive of your quest. Ask questions, learn about their culture and way of life.

- As you prepare to leave them, recognize how real this journey has been. Remind your conscious mind to recall these experiences.

- To leave, simply wish to be back in your bed. You will float up and away from this planet and in no time at all arrive back in your room. Once more, remind your conscious mind to remember every experience. Even repeat it over to your self.
- Allow your spirit body to be drawn back into your physical body. Once more inform yourself that you will wake up immediately with a clear memory of where you have been.
- Close all your chakras. Sit up and write everything down. Your memory may not have all the information; but as you write, some that has been lost may return.

50 Meditation To Increase Size & Power In The Spirit Body

When we are small children, we are made to believe that our spirit, like our physical body, is very small. As we mature, our consciousness does not include the growth of our spirit body. This meditation is designed to help you come into full realization that this body has matured too, and is in fact far larger and more powerful than your physical body and mind.

- Sit in an upright position, legs comfortably outstretched, hands resting palm up on your thighs. Close your eyes and breathe deeply.
- Become aware of your Crown Chakra and feel the center of your skull with your mind. Allow a feeling of energy to build.

- Continue to breathe slowly and deeply. Visualize this chakra oozing out a golden energy to form a large halo around the top of your head.
- Watch as this energy begins to rotate in a clockwise direction and descend down towards your Third Eye Chakra. Notice how this beautiful golden energy is forming the shape of an egg. Continue to breathe deeply.
- Observe as this energy continues on down to your Throat Chakra, then the Heart Chakra, until it reaches your Solar Plexus Chakra. Notice how the widest part of the egg shape is now formed. Breathe deeply and relax.
- Now, watch as your golden energy continues on down to your Spleen Chakra. Notice how it begins to form the slimmer part of the egg shape. Breathe slowly and relax.
- Observe your egg shape to be continuing down over your Base Chakra and on down to your feet. Your golden egg is now fully formed and encompasses you completely. Breathe slowly and accept that this is your own energy and that it has power.
- Breathe slowly and gently allow your hands to rise up towards your face. As they rise, allow yourself to physically feel this energy you have created. Sense the tingles and prickles in your hands and know that you have proved the existence of your own power.
- Breathe deeply and slowly and lower your hands to your lap.
- Now, slowly allow yourself to visualize this wonderful golden egg shape that is your spirit body. In your mind's eye, observe it expanding upwards and outward, as well as downward into the ground. Allow it to become enormous and consciously become aware of just how big your spirit body really is.
- Breathe deeply and tell yourself how big and powerful you

are in spirit and consciously accept that this body is your true self residing within your physical body. Know that you lose none of this power when it contracts to fit the physical body. Watch as your golden egg shape shrinks to fit the size of your body. Breathe deeply.

- Allow yourself to sit a while and enjoy being aware of your inner strength.
- Now, when you are ready, visualize all your Major Chakras closing from the feet upward, leaving your Crown Chakra slightly dilated. Observe this small golden blob over your head; see this as your name written in gold above your head for all to see. Breathe slowly and begin to release yourself from this meditation.
- When ready, move into a different position and consciously congratulate yourself on your growth through this meditation.

About The Author

Dr. Margaret Rogers Van Coops has been an ordained minister of the Universal Christ Church (School of Spiritualism) since 1983. She is currently the Director of Education for UCC. Dr. Margaret is a certified hypnotherapist who has practiced successfully in Spain, France, Switzerland, India, Egypt, Japan, England, Mexico and the United States. Her professional affiliations include the Spiritualist Association of Great Britain, the British Astrological and Psychic Society, The American Board of Hypnotherapy, the International Hypnosis Federation, the Professional Board of Hypnotherapy and The American Counseling Association. Dr. Margaret was among the co-founders of the International Psychic Forum and the American Metaphysical Society. She is the creator of seven therapy modalities that are collectively known as the Breakthrough Therapies: Crystal Acupuncture^{sm}, Spiritual Crystal Acupuncture^{sm}, Beauty Crystal Acupuncture^{sm}, Teragram^{sm} Therapy, Core Teragram^{sm} Therapy, TrinityStone^{sm} Therapy and Sensory Touch Therapy (STT^{sm}). Her dynamic lectures and workshops in England, Japan and the U.S. have led to regular invitations to speak and participate in international events, including Whole Life Expos and Lifeways/BMSE Expos in various American Cities and The Festivals for Mind, Body and Spirit in London and Los Angeles.

She is the author of seven metaphysically oriented texts, including *The Way to Oneness, The Rejection Syndrome, 50 Spiritually Powerful Meditations, Pro-Life, Pro-Choice, Pro-Spirit, Breakthrough Therapies: Crystal Acupuncture^{sm} & Teragram^{sm} Therapy, The Book of Crystal Acupuncture^{sm} & Teragram^{sm} Therapy Diagrams, and Expanding Images with The OmniCard^{sm}*. She has authored two novels: *Regenesis and Henry's Secrets*. Her books have been published in Western and Eastern Europe as well as Russia, China, Mexico and India. Dr. Margaret has written screenplays including *The Regenesis Trilogy, Seeing Blind* and *The Survivor*, and she is negotiating production of several reality TV series treatments. Dr. Margaret's TV series, Psychic Chit Chat, has been aired weekly on many public access channels in Southern California and Arizona. The show features Dr. Margaret and her husband, Dr. Stephen Michael Van Coops, also a Metaphysician and collaborator on her works.

PRODUCTS AND SERVICES FROM SUMARIS ENTERPRISES

THERAPY KITS

Dr. Margaret's Crystal Acupuncture℠ Therapy Kit

This amazing set contains 8 crystals and 3 pendulums attractively packaged in a satin purse, which can be easily carried in a handbag or pocket. Included in the kit is a booklet of *Crystal Acupuncture℠* diagrams. This clear and detailed work gives directions on the use of the points and pendulums and also presents valuable information on the Chakras, the Five Bodies and the acupuncture meridians.

Dr. Margaret's Teragram℠ Therapy Kit

Dispel the Madness with our kit containing one each of Natural, Blue, Violet, Red, Green and Pink Agate plates attractively contained in a satin drawstring pouch. A simple instruction booklet provides directions and tips. As a special bonus, we include a CD by Dr. Margaret Rogers Van Coops with a color meditation and a meditation for Chakra and Five Bodies balancing.

Dr. Margaret's "Core" Teragram℠ Therapy Kit

Releases Negative History stored in your body's cells. Banishes effects of old issues. Strengthens you to deal with emotional and mental issues. Stimulates more efficient energy flow. Generates inner sense of well-being. Dr. Margaret Rogers Van Coops' *"Core" Teragram℠ Therapy Kit* contains 3 specially selected Agate slices with a Basic Relaxation Meditation CD featuring the nurturing voice of Dr. Stephen Van Coops. You will quickly enter into a deep alpha state ideal for releasing old emotional habits and irrelevant mind conditioning.

Dr. Margaret's Spiritual Crystal Acupuncture℠ Kit

Five small triangular stones combined with four specially selected pointed stones to refine dense energy and to redirect it according to your desire or need. Kit includes detailed booklet with instructions and diagrams. Spiritual Geometry leads to focus on Spiritual reality beyond your previous physical awareness.

Dr. Margaret's TrinityStone℠ Healing Kit

This unique kit allows auditory memory to stimulate and shift negativity from the body. The five specially selected large open equilateral triangles are used on the Chakras, one at a time, and then all together to erase fear and illusions stored in associations with sounds. Each triangle, when added, will enhance your perception, vision and positive sensations. Included is a booklet with instructions and diagrams and two Serpentine isosolese triangles that are useful in raising the Kundalini and stimulating and harmonizing the Higher and Lower Sacred Centers. When all seven triangles are used together, an awakening may be realized that will result in an explosion of self-confidence.

BOOKS

*Breakthrough Therapies: Crystal Acupuncture*sm *& Teragram*sm *Therapy*

While most people today vaguely realize that the body is a working machine that generates energy, most of us do not understand the way that energy flows, where it goes, and what it does. ***Breakthrough Therapies*** is the product of Dr. Margaret's research with her clients and under medical supervision. Her research has validated the integration of the energies of The Five Bodies. The book reveals how the principles of Oriental Acupuncture, combined with the use of specially cut crystals and semi-precious stones, will unblock energy flow in our Five Bodies and will tone, stimulate and balance the Chi energies. Using natural resonating energy stones and crystals such as, but not limited to Hematite, Jasper, Citrine, Amethyst, Carnelian and Quartz, has opened the door to drug-free, inexpensive solutions to emotional and psychological issues ranging from addictions to depression to stress. Dr. Margaret's powerful, non-invasive healing methods also provide remarkable relief from minor physical ailments like headaches to major illnesses and syndromes such as AIDS, Cancer and Multiple Sclerosis. Author House Publishing Co.

The Way to Oneness

This inspiring work delves into the cosmology of multi-dimensional spiritual existence. Beginning with the "Word" as vibrational consciousness, this book takes you on a journey through the principles of creation, separation, the descending and ascending currents, faith, intuition, belief and evolution. The various sub-divisional cosmologies of the seven archetypes and planes of existence are viewed. Also, incarnation, reincarnation and the Akashic Records are explained as an inter-relationship with the deep subconscious and the Chakras. Of particularly unique interest is the principle of soul fragmentation that the book discusses throughout the text. ***The Way to Oneness*** concludes with practical steps and techniques for emotional balancing and relaxation, disciplinary exercises and various other psychic tools such as astrology, numerology, graphology and palmistry. Recommended for all practitioners seeking insight into higher knowledge.

— *James Ravenscroft* Whole Life Times *March 15, 1990*

The Rejection Syndrome

In our daily lives, all of us experience moments of rejection that create an internal impasse, either by ourselves or by others. My intent is to assist those wishing to be free of those encumbrances brought about by ***The Rejection Syndrome***. This is about a pattern of existence that compounds habit, routine and conditioning, leading to limitation, restriction, judgment and competition. Learn about the soul structure and how you can use it to be aware of yourself and to perform to the best of your ability without negativity or rejection.

50 Spiritually Powerful Meditations

In the stillness of the mind lies the answer to your purpose. Dr. Margaret has tested all of these meditations herself. By doing each of these meditations, you can find true direction for your life and release fears, pains, restrictions and anger acquired through conditioning. These meditations work! Develop your psychic ability, fine tune your healing skills, mend relationships, empower yourself and much more. This should be a book on everyone's shelf.

Pro-Life, Pro-Choice, Pro-Spirit

Spirit's truth is clearly shown through Dr. Margaret's own personal experiences. Is everything pre-ordained? The word "abortion" evokes emotions in almost all normally rational minds. Right or wrong? Moral or immoral? Should it be legal or illegal? One of the most burning issues of our time: Advocates of both sides have thrown themselves at each other's faces even to the point of violence. This book is a must read for women who have been, are now or are likely to become pregnant. Without being judgmental, Dr. Margaret provides the wisdom of Master Teachers to assist women to acknowledge, accept and deal with their circumstances. She has crossed the worldly boundaries to discover just what really happens from the point of view of the child-to-be's Spirit and Spirit Master Teachers.

FOCUSING TOOL

The OmniCard[sm]

The OmniCard[sm] is the newest, simplest way of doing a psychic reading for yourself, your friends or your clients. This revolutionary tool lets you easily tap into images that apply to the question being asked. This can be a wonderful new adventure in learning and psychic awareness. Simply attune to a question and then let your eyes scan the images until one looms up at you. Visualize the significance of the image and all of the meanings it draws forth. It's like having an entire Tarot deck of cards in one stylistic full-color painting, which evokes vivid, literal and symbolic images. These images are the focal points for you to create a psychic reading that will entertain and amaze your friends and clients. Try closing your eyes and letting your hand move over the OmniCard. Your fingers may point to some image of interest or significance. There are many ways to interpret the answers to questions. Try experimenting with them and discover how effective you can be. Special bonus! We are including ***Expanding Images,*** a special book and glossary of symbols with your OmniCard that will make it even easier for you to match the pictures with their meanings.

EDUCATIONAL TOOLS

Audio Tapes & CD's

Dr. Margaret Rogers Van Coops has given many informative and interesting lectures, which are available on audiocassettes. Dr Margaret has also recorded powerful meditations and hypnosis inductions which are available on CD's. Please contact Sumaris Enterprises for titles and prices.

Personal Services

Dr. Margaret is available for private consultations and is also available to do audiotaped readings by mail or over the phone. Call: (928) 453-7974

Price information can be obtained from Sumaris Enterprises. Please allow for $7.50 S&H for each item order in the United States. $15.00 S&H for Overseas orders. Arizona residents must add 8.00% for sales tax. Visa, Master, Amex and Discovery Cards accepted. All orders to be in US Dollars or equivalent amount.
Send orders with correct amount to:

Sumaris Enterprises
321 Farallon Dr., Lake Havasu City, AZ 86403, USA.
Website: www.sumariscenter.com
e-mail: sumariscenter@gmail.com